SOUTHWEST BY
◈SOUTHWEST◈

Also by Kirstin Olsen

Quilter's Color Workbook, Unlimited Designs from Easy-to Make Quilt Blocks

Remember the Ladies, A Woman's Book of Days

SOUTHWEST BY ◇SOUTHWEST◇

Native American and Mexican Designs for Quilters

Kirstin Olsen

A Sterling/Main Street Book
Sterling Publishing Co., Inc.   New York

Library of Congress Cataloging-in-Publication Data

Olsen, Kirstin.
Southwest by southwest : native American and Mexican designs for
quilters / Kirstin Olsen.
    p.   cm.
"A Sterling/Main Street book."
Includes bibliographical references (p.   ) and index.
ISBN 0-8069-7439-7 (trade).—ISBN 0-8069-7438-9 (pbk.)
1. Quilting—Patterns. 2. Quilts—Themes, motives. 3. Indians of North
America—Art. 4. Indians of Mexico—Art. I. Title.   90-23691
   TT835.048 1991   CIP
   746.9'7—dc20

Design by John Murphy
Typeset by Upper Case Ltd., Cork, Ireland

10 9 8 7 6 5 4 3 2 1

A Sterling/Main Street Book

Text © 1991 by Kirstin Olsen
Illustrations © 1991 by Sterling Publishing Company, Inc.
Published by Sterling Publishing Company, Inc.
387 Park Avenue South, New York, N.Y. 10016
Distributed in Canada by Sterling Publishing
% Canadian Manda Group, P.O. Box 920, Station U
Toronto, Ontario, Canada M8Z 5P9
Distributed in Great Britain and Europe by Cassell PLC
Villiers House, 41/47 Strand, London WC2N 5JE, England
Distributed in Australia by Capricorn Ltd.
P.O. Box 665, Lane Cove, NSW 2066

Sterling   ISBN 0-8069-7438-9/paper
            ISBN 0-8069-7439-7/trade

CONTENTS

PREFACE

THUMB THROUGH ANY quilting book and it is likely that you will encounter patterns familiar to almost every quilter — double nine patch, turkey tracks, drunkard's path, Ohio star, lone star, and so on. These traditional designs are like old friends, comfortable, well-known, and well-loved. But sometimes we yearn for something new. Experienced quilters often satisfy this desire by creating picture quilts of surpassing artistry — and difficulty. What happens to those of us trapped between these alternatives? What happens to those of us who, on the one hand, are bored with the same old patterns and who, on the other hand, are uncertain of our ability to create a masterpiece unaided?

One answer comes from a reexamination of the history of quilting. The quilt patterns we all know and loved moved, like the women who created and sustained them, across North America from east to west. They are, for the most part, the products of a European culture. However, the United States today is enriched by a wide variety of cultural influences, each with its own principles of design and color.

When I moved to the West Coast, I was startled to find that there was not a single house like the one I grew up in, not a single street like my street at "home." The trees, the land, the people, and the architecture were alien to me. I quickly became accustomed to California, but I noticed that as I did so my ideas about design changed slightly. I saw new landscapes, new colors, new motifs, and I began to think about putting them into quilts. My "new" designs were derived from the world around me, just as the eastern quilts once were, but the differences between East and West were noticeable.

The design motifs seen every day in the West — on buildings, furnishings, blankets, advertisements, and even license plates —owe an enormous debt to the visions of Native American artists. Many of these patterns, coming as they do from a tradition that emphasizes the geometric and the abstract, lend themselves well to quilting. Bold, bright, and dramatic, they are perfect for the quilter looking for something different.

This book attempts to accomplish two goals — to familiarize those who have little knowledge of southwestern design with its history and principles, and to provide instructions for quilt projects in this genre. I hope you find these projects as intriguing, satisfying, and attractive as I have. Happy quilting!

Kirstin Olsen
Mountain View, California

7

INTRODUCTION

WHILE NOT ALL SOUTHWESTERN art can be easily adapted for quilting, it is surprising how much of it can. The Native American civilizations of Arizona, California, New Mexico, and Mexico used (and still use) colors and motifs in their artwork which lend themselves well to quilting. The most popular colors are numerous and varied, yet distinctly southwestern in flavor. Many designs are highly stylized or geometric, making them easy to adapt. And the media used by southwestern artists often have advantages and limitations similar to those offered by quilting.

Native American art in the United States, even in only the small area of the United States with which we are concerned, encompasses the work of many cultures. Even within a single culture, there is astounding variety. In the Navajo nation alone, for example, there are over a dozen major regional weaving styles, ranging from the simple striped designs of Chinle to the complex oriental-style rugs of Two Grey Hills.

This "Sand Painting" weaving (right), *so named because it is a permanent version of the Southwest's transitory paintings of colored sand, uses four different colors for the four cardinal directions. Southwest Museum Collection.*

Fran Soika, one of the most talented makers of Southwest-style quilts in the United States, was inspired by Sand Painting weaving to create the Sand Painting quilt above, 31" x 39".

Opposite page: A Pueblo sampler quilt, 66" x 88", made in 1982 by a class under the direction of Californian Roberta Horton, retains authentic patterns and a bold orange-and-brown color scheme. Photo, Tony Henning.

Southwestern Indians have also worked in a number of media, including jewelry, ceramics, sand paintings, textiles, and basketry. Sand paintings and jewelry often have very complex patterns; ambitious quilters have adapted these for appliqué quilts. Such designs can also be simplified or used as quilting patterns, but on the whole they do not yield the best inspiration for block-based quilts.

The best quilt ideas often come from textiles, pottery, and basketry. Pots and baskets frequently have one simple design in a band around the opening. These patterns are often perfect for quilting or pieced blocks. More complex designs, often circular because of the shape of the vessel, make good quilting medallions. Rugs and blankets, because

The terraced basket is a classic example of Chemehuevi work. Southwest Museum Collection.

they bear the greatest resemblance to quilts in shape and size, are the best source of ideas for overall patterns, especially if one large design rather than a block-by-block construction is desired. These vary widely from one tribe to another, and within tribes by location or the style of the artist.

Navajo textiles are perhaps the best known, partly because of their superior quality and partly because they were some of the first to be marketed on a large scale to tourists. In addition, the traditional methods of weaving are lost in some tribes for various reasons. In the case of San Ildefonso Pueblo in New Mexico, the last weaver died in 1887. In Zuni villages, white encroachment meant, among other things, that the simple black blankets woven for ceremonies and used as shrouds were replaced by commercially-produced items.

The classic Navajo styles include Chinle and Two Grey Hills, mentioned above, as well as Crystal, Burntwater, Storm Pattern, Teec Nos Pos, and Wide Ruins. Crystal rugs are usually either oriental-style with two or three large, dominant symbols (often accompanied by swastikas and arrows), or simpler in design, featuring wavy stripes. They are usually executed in combinations of black, gray, white, red, brown, and gold. Storm Pattern designs are similar to quilts in that they are divided into sections, usually rectangular, each of which has its own particular pattern. Teec Nos Pos textiles are done entirely in muted browns, grays, and white with black outlining and occasional splashes of red. The patterns are often quite complex, as are those of Burntwater rugs. Wide Ruins blankets are executed entirely in pastels. Woven without borders, they consist simply of a great number of horizontal bands or stripes.

These Hopi spiral plaques rest on a dramatic blanket patterned with irregular terraced diamonds. Southwest Museum Collection.

Hopi weaving is also well known and highly esteemed. Unlike Navajo work, it remained largely uninfluenced by European methods and materials until well into this century. Traditional designs, techniques, and colors have therefore been well preserved. In fact, much of the influence of the European invaders has been removed from Hopi weaving; for example, commercial blue dyes used in the early twentieth century were replaced in the late 1920s by natural indigo.

Men do almost all of the weaving in Hopi villages, either at home or in groups with other men. (This division of labor is not unusual, though in many Native American cultures, such as the Navajo, it is the women who do most of the weaving.) Hopi blankets are often much simpler in color than their Navajo counterparts. They are predominantly white, gray, black, and dark brown. However, it is not simply the weaving itself that makes Hopi textiles so unique. Once the blanket is complete, wide bands of embroidery are added, frequently in black, green, or red. Geometric in design, often featuring groups of triangles and diamond-shaped inserts, these bands are one of the most recognizable and characteristic Hopi motifs. The finished blanket is a masterpiece of contrast.

One of the most interesting of the Hopi blankets is the bride's dress. It begins its life as a simple white blanket, unadorned by decoration of any kind. After the wedding, the embroidery is added in black and green, with details in several colors. What makes this garment so fascinating, other than its use as a wedding dress, is its *real* purpose — to make certain that its wearer can pass to the afterlife when she dies. As such, it is the most essential piece of clothing in a Hopi woman's life.

Fran Soika adapted these thunderbirds for wall hangings. The technique in which one of the birds faces the "wrong" way comes straight from the original Native American artwork. Shown in color is "The Gathering," 94" x 56", and, in black-and-white, "Thunderbirds," 58" x 17".

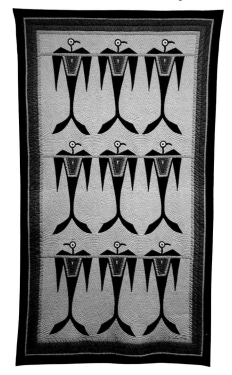

A more complex thunderbirds design by Soika resembles a shield or a coat of arms. It is 54" x 64".

This double-spouted Pueblo jar features birds in its design. Southwest Museum Collection.

Different Indian groups had favorite subjects or colors. Birds, for example, were particularly important in Pueblo art, while the Zuni favored abstract designs. The Yuma of the Mohave desert often portrayed the sun, moon, and stars, and the Acoma were fond of trees, leaves, birds, and flowers. The significance of colors, too, differs from one culture to another. In Zuni art, yellow stands for the north, red for the south, blue for the west, and white for the east. In Navajo art,

Birds are a common motif on Pueblo pottery, and in this quilt, seen overall and in two details, Fran Soika has united nine different birds from nine different Pueblo sources.

Zuni pottery makes use of complicated geometric figures and animal and bird motifs. Southwest Museum Collection.

however, black is associated with the north and yellow with the south. (East and west are the same as for the Zuni.) Of course, the cardinal directions are not the only things symbolized by color. In Yuman art, a white background indicates honor or glory in battle. Red stands for military achievement, sunset, or thunder. Green symbolizes grass or summer, and yellow the sun, war horses, or dawn.

Abstract Zuni rain birds by Fran Soika. Left, 34" x 37"; right, 35" square.

Feathers and arrows are common motifs in almost all Native American art, though sometimes they are hardly recognizable as feathers or arrows to the uninitiated. Some ancient Hopi feather designs found on pottery, for example, appear to be nothing more than diamonds or squares with prongs to the right and left. After glancing at a few of these patterns, one is tempted to call anything with lines or points on it a feather. This, however, is a dangerous assumption. Designs that look like one group's feathers may be another group's arrows or birds. Explication can become quite confusing. Further complications arise when one realizes that clouds and rain, too, are common motifs, and those lines or points, if vertical rather than horizontal, may indicate rainfall.

A detail from Fran Soika's celebrated Acoma quilt shows how she has reproduced an almost impossibly intricate design.

History can also influence the appearance of the weaving. Chief blankets, described below, went through four distinct phases of development, and so a blanket woven in 1810 would be completely unlike one woven in the same region in 1880. European invaders also had a strong influence on Native American weaving. They brought new dyes and new motifs — many nineteenth-century Navajo rugs incorporate such alien elements as food labels, American flags, and letters of the English alphabet.

Despite this vast, immeasurable variety, however, there are some themes in Native American art which are more popular than others. While the interpretation may differ, the message is frequently the same. Two underlying themes pervade much of the native art of the Southwest — the complexity of the world, and the continuity or universality of its parts.

A Pueblo sash relies on embroidery and not weaving for its intricate decoration. Southwest Museum Collection.

There are also some patterns which are particularly common in the region. One of these classic designs is the banded rug or blanket. Colored with vegetal dyes that yield soft pastels and earth tones, it consists of several parallel horizontal bands, one on top of another. The bands are sometimes wide, sometimes narrow, sometimes straight, sometimes broken into a herringbone pattern, but the basic theme is repeated over and over in Native American textiles.

Perhaps the best-known Navajo pattern is the "chief blanket," so called because originally these blankets were worn by individuals of great status. Chief blankets have contrasting vertical bands in vivid colors. The later blankets have large diamonds and triangles or crosses in the centers and running off the sides. They are predominantly rendered in combinations of red, black, blue, and white. (A Navajo chief blanket is the inspiration for the quilt project in chapter 2 of this book).

Some Native American blankets are highly complex. After European settlers exposed local artists to Asian designs, there was an explosion of "orientalized" rugs with complicated, often binary, central designs and elaborate borders. The best of these rugs are usually woven in combinations of black, white, gray, ivory, slate blue, brown, and a uniquely deep, rich red known as "Ganado red."

During the late nineteenth century, new dyes and the interest of poorly educated tourists gave rise to "eye dazzler" blankets. These pieces were full of many bright colors juxtaposed in a rather gaudy and often unpleasant fashion. Fortunately, artists returned to simpler color schemes, using only a few strong colors (often primaries) or several muted ones. The "eye dazzler" combinations, while legitimately part of southwestern art, are usually less than highly regarded, and quilters should think twice before copying them.

Ideally, from a quilter's perspective, the motifs in Native American textiles, basketry, and pottery are usually highly stylized. Humans, animals, and plants are often represented, but frequently they cannot be recognized by those unfamiliar with the symbols used. These symbols

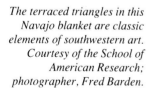

The terraced triangles in this Navajo blanket are classic elements of southwestern art. Courtesy of the School of American Research; photographer, Fred Barden.

This Mexican blanket (detail) makes use of the ancient Mayan calendar motif. Southwest Museum Collection.

vary widely, and a thorough explanation of them is beyond the scope of this book. A little research, however, will reveal that certain shapes, such as terraced pyramids, are common throughout southwestern art. These are also immediately recognizable to most people and can create a southwestern atmosphere quite effectively.

ART FROM SOUTH of the border is similar in many respects to that of Arizona, New Mexico, and California. Many of the same colors — primaries and desert hues — are associated with this region, and geometric motifs and stylized figures are also extremely common. However, secondary colors, such as orange and green, are more commonly associated with Mexico than with the southwestern United States, and certain patterns common in Mexican artifacts are not found farther north. For example, the ancient Mayans carved highly complex portraits of their gods. These bizarre, fascinating shapes with their intricate curves would make exquisite quilting patterns for a very ambitious, very patient artist. There are also some motifs which, while they are found on both sides of the border, are more commonly associated with Mexican art — such as Christian symbols.

Mexican artists, like artists in the United States, have created beautiful textiles from which quilters can draw inspiration, but in many cases there are different media available to give us ideas.. Many of the native civilizations which flourished before the European invasion were builders. They left not only jewelry, textiles, and pottery, but also toys, architecture, statuary, stamps for marking clay, and other artifacts. Toys and statuary are of limited use to the quilter, but friezes from buildings and stamps meant to be rolled over clay often provide good patterns for border quilting and pieced blocks. Their subjects include not only gods and unusual repetitions of shapes but also snakes, owls, eagles, hummingbirds, flowers, feathers, jaguars, bats, monkeys, wooden rattles used in dances, shells, games, arrows, flags, the sun, crosses, corn, insects, butterflies, fish, toads, lizards, and the "blue worm" — an S-shaped scroll which represents a constellation or a sceptre. Many of these depictions are quite elaborate; like the carvings of the Mayan gods they are best for very patient quilters. The simple designs, however, can be adapted for pieced blocks with very little difficulty.

NOT ALL OF THE quilts based on southwestern art are derived from Native American or Mexican art. Some are based on the invaders' visions of the landscape. These quilts are less abstract. They tend not to be composed of pieced blocks; rather, they are overall designs, usually appliquéd, and frequently far more intricate and difficult than block quilts.

Many aspects of the Southwest can serve as inspirations for such quilts. The distinctive adobe architecture of the region evokes an immediate sense of place, as do the ancient terraced pyramids of

Fran Soika created this quilt, 24" x 36", for the Santa Fe Trading Company in Cleveland, Ohio. The stark white of the adobe and the brilliant blue of the sky are in perfect contrast.

Mexico. The desert landscape, too, is uniquely identifiable. Gently sloping mountains, sheer striated cliffs, deep canyons, tall spindly fingers of rock and precariously balanced boulders make splendid subjects, as do the brilliant desert sky, the earth, and vivid western sunsets. No one artist yields so many excellent ideas as Georgia O'Keeffe. Her long love affair with the Southwest is reflected in her work, and if all else fails you in your search for a landscape to quilt, locate some reproductions of her paintings. Her use of color, bold and dramatic images, and archetypal symbols of the Southwest will very likely give you a good starting place.

At first one notices the odd balloon floating above the desert landscape in Fran Soika's "Pineapple Circus" quilt, 53" x 41" (right). *Only on closer inspection* (below left), *does one see that those "flowers" on the cacti are actually* cans *of pineapple.*

Below right: *The olive background of Fran Soika's Tsia Rain Birds quilt, 43" x 45", calls to mind the colors of cacti.*

Much of the plant life of the Southwest can be incorporated into quilts with excellent results. Unmistakably symbolic of the region, the hundreds of varieties of cactus, especially the huge "armed" saguaro, offer interesting and easily recognizable shapes to the quilter. Pointy, many-leafed yuccas are also intriguing. Tumbleweeds might seem impossible to portray, but a general shape can be appliquéd and the details quilted in a contrasting color. Cactus spines can also be quilted or created by tufts.

Stylized birds and deer populate this quilt by Fran Soika entitled "Great Lakes," 22" x 44". Note the one deer which faces away from the others.

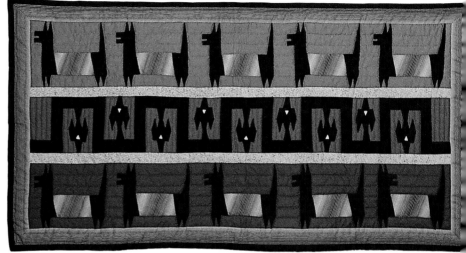

Animal life abounds in the Southwest, and some of it has already been mentioned above. Birds of all kinds survive there, though some, like the inevitable roadrunner, are particularly characteristic. (The ancient Mexicans knew the roadrunner as the "shouting pheasant.") Snakes, lizards, and other reptiles inhabit the desert, as do rabbits, scorpions, coyotes, and other small creatures. The more exotic creatures include the jaguar (associated largely with Mexico) and the mountain lion or puma.

Of course, human animals also inhabit the region. For the truly ambitious, re-creating the movement and color of a Mexican outdoor market can be a thoroughly enjoyable challenge. Pueblo villages, Hopi kachina dances, and celebrations and everyday tasks of all kinds make good subjects. For those who want to evoke what some call the Old West, there are other scenes to consider as well. Try your hand at ghost towns, cowboys, cattle drives, covered wagons, coal-driven locomotives, saloons, stagecoaches, and Pony Express riders.

Californian Mary Jo Hill made these whimsical "Jack rabbit Crossing" quilts. Design courtesy of Piecemakers Country Store.

Blanche Young's humorous "Lone Star" quilt mixes the piecing patterns of a traditional eastern design with the West's own Lone Ranger.

Here Fran Soika pairs traditional terraced diamonds with nineteenth-century trains in a Navajo-style wall hanging, 46" x 54".

The journey from inspiration to finished quilt is often an arduous one filled with frustration as well as delight. Three of the design projects that I undertook illustrate both the challenge and the pleasure of accomplishment which is experienced. In the case of the "Chief Blanket" pattern (chapter 2), there was more delight than frustration. Chief blankets are common enough, and it was merely a matter of finding the best single variation. It was found not in a photograph of a blanket, but in a 1928 painting, "Santo," by Ramond Jonson. The checkerboard pattern made it especially easy to adapt for piecing. The

*"Santo," by Ramond Jonson,
1928, oil on canvas, 40" x 28".
Courtesy of the Roswell
Museum and Art Center,
Roswell, New Mexico.*

only difficulty lay in extrapolating the rest of the design from the small
portion shown in the painting, but the availability of other chief
blankets made that a relatively simple task.

In the case of the "Pyramids" pattern (chapter 3), however, the
process was not so easy. The original plan was to reproduce as much as
possible of the painting, "Buffalo Hunt" by Ma-Pe-Wi. Ultimately,
however, because of the difficulty of that task, the quilt focused on one
tiny detail — the row of terraced pyramids at the bottom of the painting.
Reducing these pyramids to quilt blocks was simple. Finding fabrics
that matched the colors in the original artwork was not. In the end, the
quilt shown in this book was made with a purple that's not *quite* the
right shade.

"Hopi" (chapter l) was perhaps the most difficult design to adapt. It
was here, more than anywhere else, that the differences between the
two media caused problems. Weaving is often difficult enough to
reproduce in quilt form, but Hopi mantas are even more complex
because their intricate patterns are not created by weaving but by
embroidery. In the end the design was simplified quite a bit and a
variety of techniques used to approximate the effect of Hopi stitchery.

"Buffalo Hunt" by Ma-Pe-Wi. Courtesy of the School of American Research.

"Crucita, A Taos Indian Girl" by Joseph Henry Sharp. Courtesy Thomas Gilcrease Institute of the American History and Art.

Those who choose to create their own southwestern quilt designs should remember that the end result doesn't always look exactly like the original piece of artwork on which it is based. And, of course, creating one's own patterns is always hard work. But the results can be spectacular and the process rewarding and challenging.

The imagery of the Southwest lends itself well to the art of quilting. Here is ample material to be adapted, whether a simple, abstract design or a complex, naturalistic pattern is the goal. In many ways, quilting based on the art of the Southwest is more flexible than traditional quilting. Traditional patterns, like traditions of any kind, can be comforting and familiar, but they can also chafe at times. The Southwest offers artists who work in fabric and thread an opportunity to be outrageous, bold, different, and pioneering. So experiment! The design projects which follow may give you some ideas, some starting points, but don't feel confined by them. The best part of learning anything new is getting to strike out on your own.

HOPI

This quilt is a synthesis of many Hopi weavings, including wedding dresses, mantas (wide wearing blankets), and the kilts worn by kachina dancers. The black rectangle-and-triangle combinations along the sides are among the most common motifs in Hopi weaving. Sometimes the stitching details on the black surfaces are done in green.

Vital Statistics

Maker: Kirstin Olsen
Length: 90" (229 cm)
Width: 70" (178 cm)
Fabric Requirements: (45" or 114 cm wide)

3 yards (3 m) black fabric
3 yards (3 m) ivory fabric
$^1/_4$ yard (23 cm) white fabric
$^1/_8$ yard (12 cm) red fabric
$5^1/_2$ yards (5 m) backing fabric

Binding: self-bound

Instructions

1. Cut all pieces. You will need:

Black
30 large triangles (6" on longest side)
20 1" x 10" strips
20 1" x 4$^1/_2$" strips
10 1" x 3$^1/_2$" strips
10 1" x 5$^1/_2$" strips
10 8" x 10" rectangles
26 11" x 2" strips
2 5" x 2" strips
20 1" x 7" strips
4 1" x 17" strips

Ivory
20 2" x 10" strips
5 16" x 14" rectangles
10 7" x 12" rectangles
4 1" x 17" strips
2 2" x 28" strips
12 2" x 11" strips
18 2" x 10" strips
20 7" (on longest side) trapezoids – 10 "right" and 10 "left" (flip template over)
20 4" (on longest side) trapezoids – 10 "right" and 10 "left" (flip template over)

White
10 triangles (5" on longest side)
20 very small triangles (1$^1/_2$" on longest side)

Red
20 small triangles (2$^1/_2$" on longest side)
20 small trapezoids (2$^1/_2$" on longest side)

25

Black   **Ivory**   **White**   **Red**

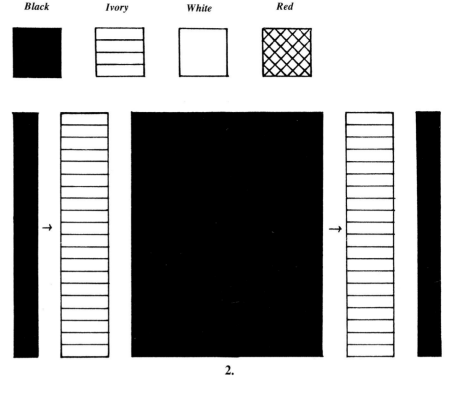

(Note: In this quilt, the red pieces have been divided in half – half are a solid red, and half are red with small white stars. You may choose to use this variation if you like, but all instructions will be given as if all pieces are solid red.)

2. Assemble the base of each block:

Sew a 1" x 10" black strip to a 2" x 10" ivory strip along the 10" sides. Repeat. Sew one black-and-ivory combination to each side of a black 8" x 10" rectangle, joining the 10" ivory side to a 10" black side.

2.

3. Assemble the top row of each block:

Sew a large ivory trapezoid to each side of a large black triangle so that the slanted sides meet and that the three pieces form a 3" x 14" strip.

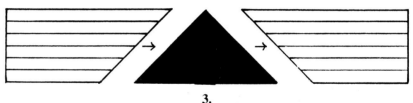

3.

4. Assemble the central diamonds:

(a) Sew a small white triangle to a red trapezoid along the trapezoid's side. Repeat. You should now have two small red-and-white triangles. Place them with the red sides facing "south."

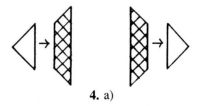

4. a)

(b) Attach red triangles to the "right" side of one red-and-white triangle and the "left" side of the other. You should now have two slightly larger triangles.

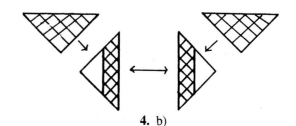

4. b)

(c) Join them along the all-red sides.

(d) Sew the longest side to the longest side of a large white triangle. This is the heart of the diamond.

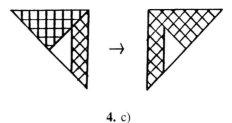

4. c)

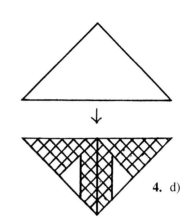

4. d)

(e) To make the perimeter, (1) sew a 1" x 3½" black strip to one side of the diamond, (2) a 1" x 4½" black strip to the next side, (3) a 1" x 4½" black strip to the next side, and (4) a 1" x 5½" black strip to make a square.

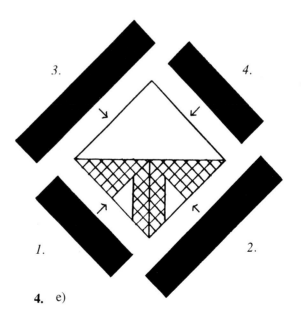

4. e)

5. Assemble the middle row of each block:

(a) Sew a large black triangle to a small "right" ivory trapezoid along the trapezoid's slanted side. Repeat with a "left" trapezoid.

5. a)

(b) Attach the opposite sides of the triangles to a central diamond. Line up the corners of the triangles with the very top of the diamond – that is, the side with the all-white triangle in it. The corners of the triangles should meet, and their sides should not be as long as the sides of the diamond. When joining the sides of the triangle and diamond, *do not stitch into your seam allowance*.

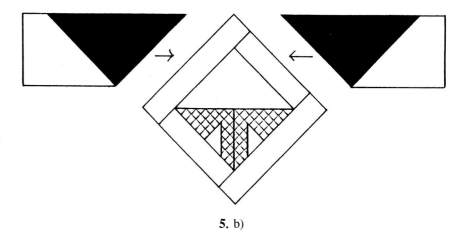

5. b)

6. Join the top row of each block to the middle row of each block.

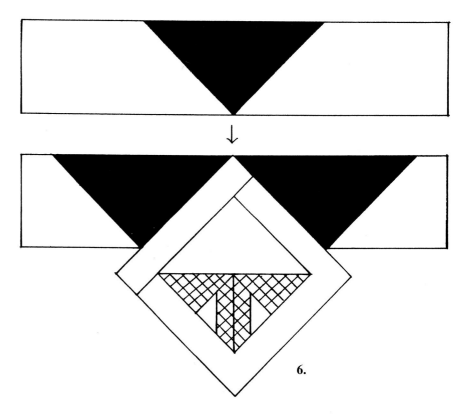

6.

7. (a) Join the top half of each block to the bottom half. *Stitch only to the point at which triangle and diamond meet.* Open and press seams.

(b) Pull the loose portion of the diamond forward, and press the seam allowance under on all of its raw edges. Pin in place. The right and left points of the diamond should meet the right and left edges of the large black rectangle. Stitch in place.

7. a)

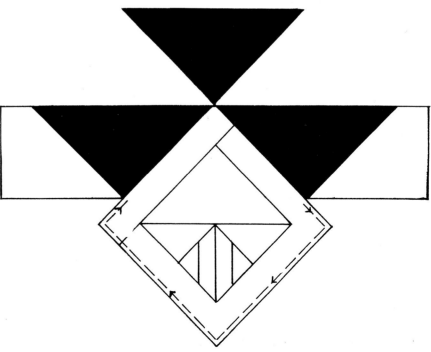

7. b)

8. Sew the blocks together in two rows of five along the 16" sides.

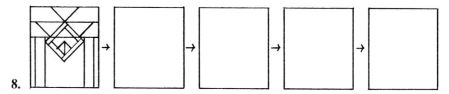

8.

9. Assemble the border blocks:

(a) Sew a 1" x 7" black strip to each short side of a 7" x 12" ivory rectangle.

(b) Join the blocks in rows of five along the black sides.

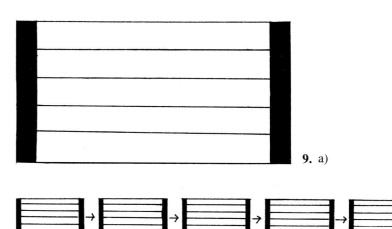

9. a)

9. b)

10. Assemble the middle panel: Join the large ivory rectangles along their 16" sides.

11. Join the blocks, border blocks, and middle panel.

12. Assemble the side strips:

(a) Sew a 1" x 17" black strip to a 1" x 17" ivory strip along the 17" sides. Repeat until you have four 2" x 17" black-and-ivory strips.

(b) Attach one to each 2" end of a 2" x 28" ivory strip, making sure that the black strips are on the same side. Repeat.

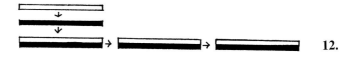

12.

13. Attach the side strips to the shorter sides of the main section, making certain the black strips line up with each other.

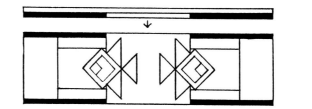

13.

14. Assemble the black border:

Sew seven 2" x 11" black strips and one 2" x 5" black strip together on their 2" sides. Repeat. Attach these to the long sides of the main section.

Sew six 2" x 11" black strips together along their 2" sides. Repeat. Attach these to the shorter sides of the quilt.

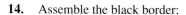

15. Assemble the ivory border:

Sew six 2" x 11" ivory strips together at their 2" ends. Repeat. Attach to the shorter sides of the quilt. Sew nine 2" x 10" strips together at their 2" ends. Repeat. Attach to the longer sides of the quilt.

16. Assemble the back:

Cut the 5½" yards of backing fabric into two 2¾-yard pieces. Attach along the long sides.

17. Pin and baste the back, batting, and top together. Trim the back, leaving about two inches beyond the top on all sides.

18. Quilting:

Begin by quilting the shield design on the middle panels. This design is adapted from a South American blanket.

Next, outline all the black areas except the 2" border.

Add the detailing in white (or green, if you prefer) on the black rectangles. Outline the areas within the diamonds.

Then do the terraced quilting in the border blocks.

Finally, outline the 2" black border. Remove basting stitches.

19. Finishing:

Fold the excess backing fabric in half, then fold again so that its edge meets the edge of the quilt. Sew in place; mitre the corners.

White details line up at bottom of large black rectangle.

Quilting Patterns

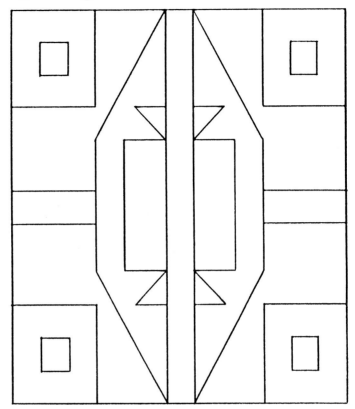

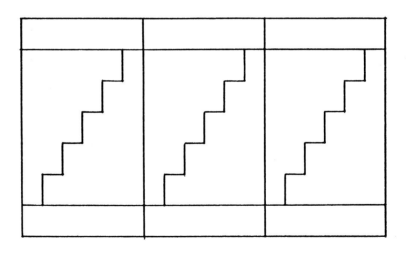

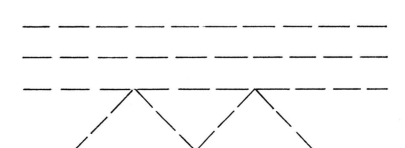

Pattern Pieces
Shown half-size unless otherwise noted

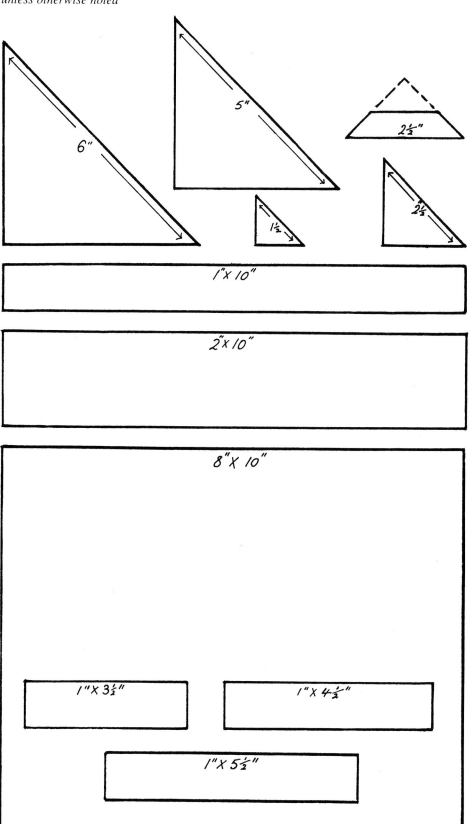

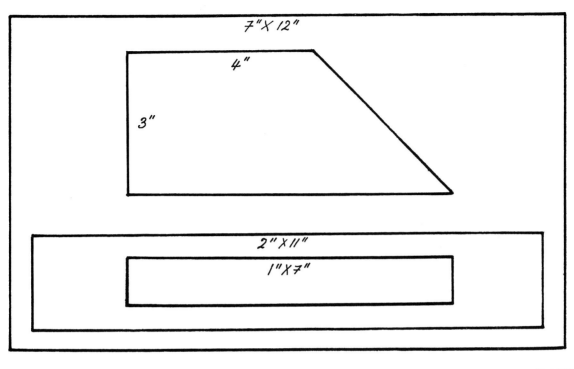

7"X 12"

4"

3"

2"X 11"

1"X 7"

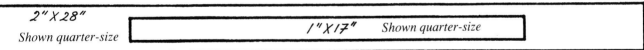

2"X 28"

Shown quarter-size

1"X 17"   *Shown quarter-size*

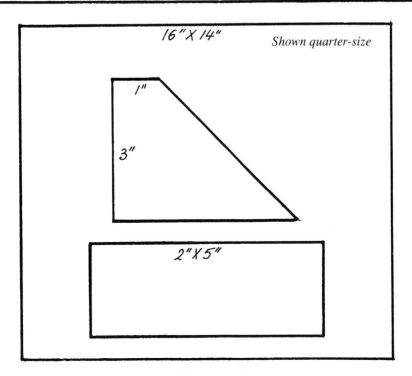

16"X 14"   *Shown quarter-size*

1"

3"

2"X 5"

CHIEF BLANKET 2

Vital Statistics

Maker: Kirstin Olsen
Length: 102" (259 cm)
Width: 90" (229 cm)
Fabric Requirements: (45" or 114 cm wide)
4 yards (3.75 m) black fabric
3¹/₂ yards (3.25 m) white fabric
2¹/₂ yards (2.3 m) red fabric
1²/₃ yards (1.5 m) blue fabric
9 yards (8.25 m) backing fabric
red bias binding or 1 extra yard of red fabric
Binding: bias-bound

Instructions

1. Cut all pieces. You will need:

Black
116 2" x 10" strips
96 2" x 6" strips

White
118 2" x 10" strips
60 2" x 6" strips

Red
369 2" x 2" squares

Blue
16 2" x 10" strips
208 2" x 2" squares

Navajo weavings known as "chief blankets" went through four distinct phases of development. Phase I blankets, woven from about 1800 to 1850, feature very wide black and white stripes, sometimes with a little indigo. In Phase II (1800-1870) red is added. Phase III (1860-1880) sees the incorporation of terraced diamonds down the middle and along the sides of the blanket. And in Phase IV (1870-1885), the diamonds begin to dominate the stripes. In very late blankets, the diamonds sometimes meet – making the stripes almost inconsequential. The chief blanket that is the subject of this project is based on a number of Phase III and Phase IV blankets. Its major virtue lies in that it is dramatic, yet deceptively simple to make.

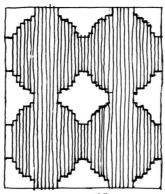

2. This quilt is assembled in vertical columns. Starting from the left-hand side of the quilt, there are 45 columns. To make the first column, sew five 2" red squares in a row; then add a blue square, a red square, and so on. Sequences for each column follow. Pieces are squares unless otherwise indicated.

3. Column #1:
5 red; 1 blue; 1 red; 1 blue; two 10" black strips; 1 blue; 1 red; 1 blue; 9 red; 1 red; 1 blue; two 10" black strips; 1 blue; 1 red; 1 blue; 5 red.

Column #2:
4 red; 1 blue; 1 red; 1 blue; 1 red; two 10" blue strips; 1 red; 1 blue; 1 red; 1 blue; 7 red; 1 blue; 1 red; 1 blue; 1 red; two 10" blue strips; 1 red; 1 blue; 1 red; 1 blue; 4 red.

Column #3:
3 red; 1 blue; 1 red; 1 blue; 1 red; four 6" black strips; 1 red; 1 blue; 1 red; 1 blue; 5 red; 1 blue; 1 red; 1 blue; 1 red; four 6" black strips; 1 red; 1 blue; 1 red; 1 blue; 3 red.

Column #4:
2 red; 1 blue; 1 red; 1 blue; one 6" white strip; two 10" white strips; one 6" white strip; 1 blue; 1 red; 1 blue; 3 red; 1 blue; 1 red; 1 blue; one 6" white strip; two 10" white strips; one 6" white strip; 1 blue; 1 red; 1 blue; 2 red.

Column #5:
1 red; 1 blue; 1 red; 1 blue; six 6" black strips; 1 blue; 1 red; 1 blue; 1 red; 1 blue; 1 red; 1 blue; six 6" black strips; 1 blue; 1 red; 1 blue; 1 red.

Column #6:
1 blue; 1 red; 1 blue; four 10" white strips; 1 blue; 1 red; 1 blue; 1 red; 1 blue; four 10" white strips; 1 blue; 1 red; 1 blue.

Column #7:
1 red; 1 blue 1 red; four 10" black strips; 1 red; 1 blue; 1 red; 1 blue; 1 red; four 10" black strips; 1 red; 1 blue; 1 red.

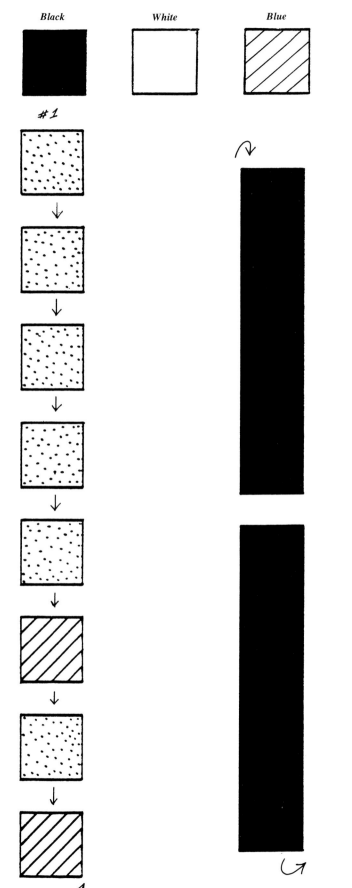

Black White Blue Red

#1

Column #8:
1 blue; 1 red; two 6" white strips; two 10" white strips; two 6" white strips; 1 red; 1 blue; 1 red; two 6" white strips; two 10" white strips; two 6"white strips; 1 red; 1 blue.

Column #9:
one 6" black strip; nine 10" black strips; one 6" black strip.

Column #10:
one 6" white strip; nine 10" white strips; one 6" white strip.

Column #11: same as #9.

Column #12: same as #10.

Column #13: same as #9.

Column #14: same as #10.

Column #15: same as #9.

Column #16: same as #8.

Column #17: same as #7.

Column #18: same as #6.

Column #19: same as #5.

Column #20: same as #4.

Column #21: same as #3.

Column #22: same as #2.

Column #23: same as #1.

Column #24: same as #2.

Column #25: same as #3.

Column #26: same as #4.

Column #27: same as #5.

Column #28: same as #6.

Column #29: same as #7.

Column #30: same as #8.

Column #31: same as #9.

Column #32: same as #10.

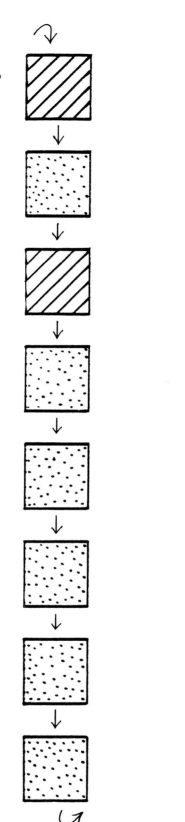

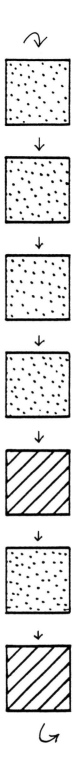

Column #33: same as #9.

Column #34: same as #10.

Column #35: same as #9.

Column #36: same as #10.

Column #37: same as #9.

Column #38: same as #8.

Column #39: same as #7.

Column #40: same as #6.

Column #41: same as #5.

Column #42: same as #4.

Column #43: same as #3.

Column #44: same as #2.

Column #45: same as #1.

4. Join the columns together in order to form the quilt top.

5. Cut the backing fabric into three 3-yard lengths. Join to form a 3-yard by 3-yard square.

6. Pin and baste back, batting, and top together. Trim backing fabric so that it is even with the top. Quilt along each column and around each blue square. Remove basting stitches.

7. Bind with bias binding.

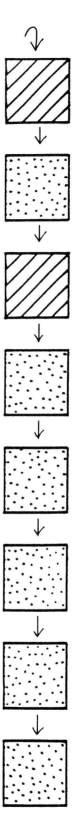

Pattern Pieces

Shown half-size

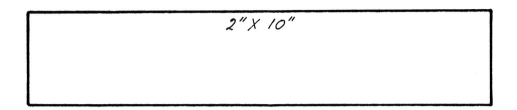

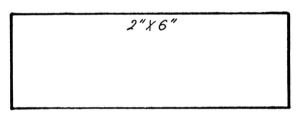

PYRAMID

3

The terraced pyramid is a common feature of southwestern art. The colors in this one were adapted from "Buffalo Hunt," a painting by Ma-Pe-Wi (Velino Shije Herrera), a Native American artist from Zia Pueblo in New Mexico.

Vital Statistics

Maker: Kirstin Olsen
Length: 105" (267 cm)
Width: 84" (213 cm)
Fabric Requirements: (45" or 114 cm wide)

$1^1/_4$ yards (1.15 m) black fabric
$4^2/_3$ yards (4.25 m) white fabric
$2^1/_2$ yards (2.25 m) blue fabric
$2^1/_2$ yards (2.25 m) yellow fabric
$1^1/_2$ yards (2 m) purple fabric
$1^1/_4$ yards (1.15 m) gray fabric
6 yards (5.5 m) backing fabric
bias binding or 1 extra yard white fabric

Binding: bias bound

Instructions

1. Cut all pieces. You will need:

Black
15 2" x 26" strips
15 triangles with a longest side of 6".

White
30 4" x 9" rectangles
30 4" x 5" rectangles
30 1" x 19" strips
30 1" x 28" strips

Blue
15 $3^1/_2$" x $3^1/_2$" squares
15 1" x 26" strips
30 trapezoids with longest side of 8"–15 "right" and 15 "left" (flip template over)

Yellow
15 $3^1/_2$" x $3^1/_2$" squares
30 trapezoids with longest side of 15"–15 "right" and 15 "left" (flip template over)

Purple
15 3" x 26" strips.

Gray
30 triangles with longest side of 7"
60 triangles with longest side of $5^1/_2$"

40

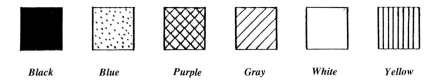

Black   *Blue*   *Purple*   *Gray*   *White*   *Yellow*

2. Assemble the base of each block:

Sew a 26" black strip to a 26" blue strip. Then attach a 26" purple strip to the other side of the blue strip.

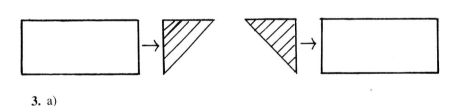

2.

3. Assemble the corners:

(a) Sew one short side of a small gray triangle to a long white rectangle. Repeat with another pair o pieces, but this time use the other short side of the triangle so that there is a "right" pair and a "left" pair.

(b) Repeat this process with two more small gray triangles and two short white rectangles.

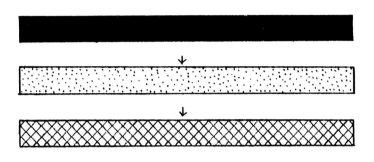

3. a)

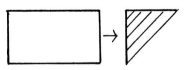 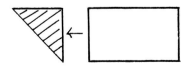

3. b)

(c) Attach each of these pairs to one of the larger pairs so that the gray triangles are on the same side.

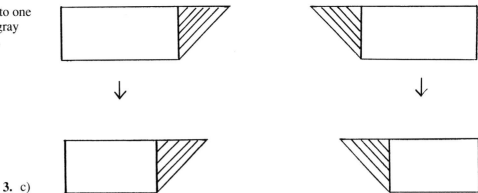

3. c)

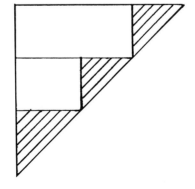

(d) Attach a large gray triangle to the bottom of each group so that a large gray-and-white triangle is formed.

3. d)

4. Assemble the center of each block:

(a) Sew the left-hand short side of a black triangle to the shorter side of a "left" blue trapezoid.

(b) Sew the 3½" side of a "right" blue trapezoid to a blue square.

(c) Attach this to the right side of the black triangle. There should now be a blue-and-black triangle.

(d) Repeat the process with the yellow trapezoids and squares so that there is an even larger triangle.

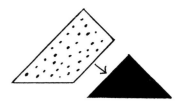

4. a)

4. b)

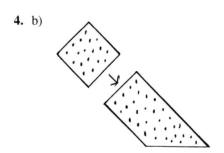

4. c)

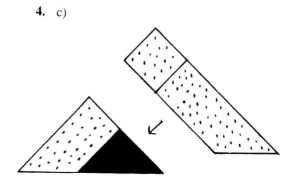

5. Assemble each block:

(a) Sew the corners, with the large gray triangles at the bottom, to the sides of the center triangle.

(b) Attach the base, with the purple side up, to the bottom of the block.

(c) Sew a 19" white strip to each of the ends of the block, and sew 28" white strips to the top and the bottom of the block.

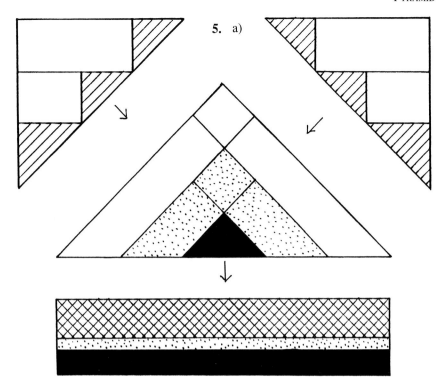

5. a)

5. b)

6. Join the blocks:

Make five rows of three and join the rows.

7. Cut the backing fabric into two three-yard lengths. Join them along their long sides. Pin and baste together the back, batting, and top. Trim backing fabric so that it is even with the top. Outline each color and block boundary with quilting. Remove basting stitches. Bind.

Pattern Pieces

Shown quarter-size

2" X 26"

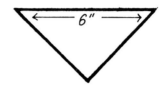

6"

4" X 9"

4" X 5"

1" X 19"

1" X 28"

$3\frac{1}{2}"X3\frac{1}{2}"$

$1"X26"$

$3"X26"$

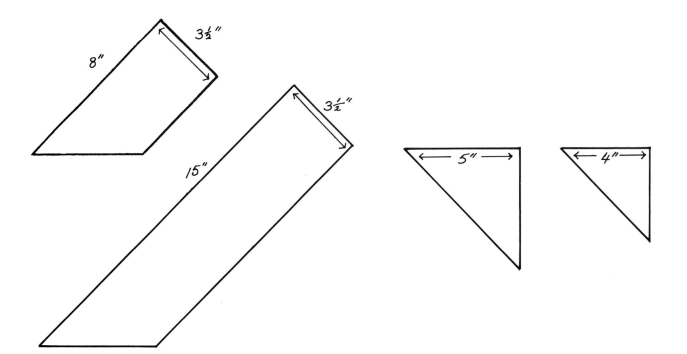

$3\frac{1}{2}"$

$8"$

$3\frac{1}{2}"$

$15"$

$5"$

$4"$

YUROK BASKET CRIB QUILT

4

Vital Statistics

Maker: Kirstin Olsen
Length: 40" (102 cm)
Width: 44" (112 cm)
Fabric Requirements: (45" or 114 cm wide)
1¹/₂ yards (1.4 m) brown fabric
²/₃ yard (.6 m) beige fabric
1¹/₄ yards (1.15 m) backing fabric bias binding or ¹/₂ yard dark brown fabric
Binding: bias bound

Instructions

1. Cut all pieces. You will need:

Brown
5   *2" x 40" strips*
8   *4" x 10" strips*
8   *2" x 10" strips*
16 *2" x 2" squares*
32 *right-angle triangles*
32 *trapezoids*

Beige
32 *trapezoids*
32 *right-angle triangles*
8 *3" x 10" strips*
16 *2" x 2" squares*

Although the Yurok are from northern California, near Mendocino, and are thus more part of the Pacific Northwest than the Southwest, Yurok patterns are frequently similar to those employed farther south. The following design, based on a Yurok basket, is very much like work done in the Southwest.

Brown   *Beige*

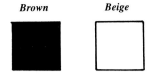

2. Assemble each block:

Each block is assembled in horizontal rows.

(a) A 2" x 10" brown strip will serve as the top row.

2.   ↓

(b) To make the second row, attach (from left to right): a brown triangle with the slanted side going from top left to bottom right; a beige trapezoid with the slanted side toward the triangle; a brown square; a beige trapezoid facing away from the square; and a brown triangle.

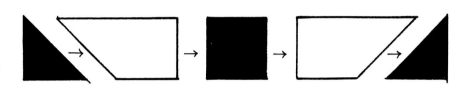

2. b)

(c) To make the third row, begin with a brown trapezoid facing the center; then add a beige triangle facing the trapezoid, a beige square, a beige triangle facing in the opposite direction, and another brown trapezoid.

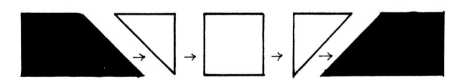

2. c)

(d) The fourth row is a 3" x 10" beige strip.

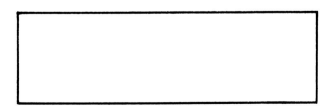

2. d)

(e) The fifth row is the same as the second with the colors reversed.

(f) The sixth row is the same as the third with the colors reversed.

(g) The bottom row is a 4" x 10" brown strip.

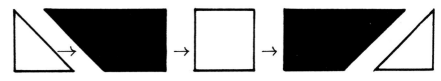

2. e)

2. f)

2. g)

3. Join the rows from top to bottom.

4. Make each row of four blocks by alternating right-side-up blocks with upside-down blocks.

Attach 2" x 40" strips to the top and bottom of the top row and to the bottom of the bottom row. Join the top and bottom rows.

Sew a 40" strip to each side of the quilt.

5. Pin and baste the back, batting, and top. Trim the backing fabric so that it is even with the top. Quilt along the outlines and around each block. Remove basting stitches. Bind.

Pattern Pieces

Shown half-size unless otherwise notea

2"X40"   *Shown at 20% of full size*

4"X10"

2"X10"

2"X2"

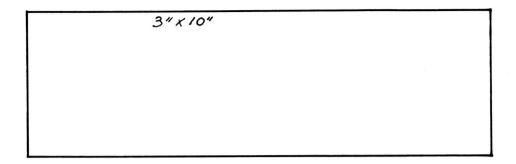

3" x 10"

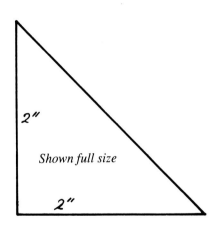

2"

Shown full size

2"

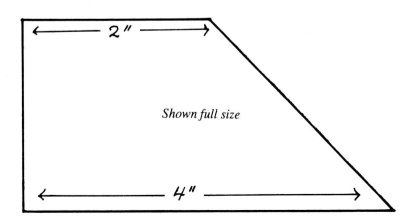

2"

Shown full size

4"

HERRINGBONE 5

While the name of this quilt may not be very characteristic of the Southwest, the pattern is. Bands of soft colors are quite common in southwestern crafts; usually the bands are straight, but this herringbone variation is also authentic–and somewhat more interesting.

Vital Statistics

Maker: Kirstin Olsen
Length: 114" (290 cm)
Width: 84" (213 cm)
Fabric Requirements: (45" or 114 cm wide)
You may wish to use different distributions of color, in which case fabric requirements may vary.

3 yards (2.75 m) brown fabric
$2^{1}/_{4}$ yards (2 m) beige fabric
$2^{1}/_{4}$ yards (2 m) patterned light-
    brown fabric
$1^{1}/_{2}$ yards (1.4 m) pink fabric
$1^{1}/_{2}$ yards (1.4 m) ivory fabric
$1^{1}/_{2}$ yards (1.4 m) green fabric
$1^{1}/_{2}$ yards (1.4 m) purple fabric
$6^{1}/_{2}$ yards backing fabric
bias binding or 1 extra yard of brown
    fabric

Binding: bias bound

Instructions

1. Cut all pieces. You will need:

Purple
16 "E" pieces–8 right and 8 left (flip
    template over)
8   "B" pieces –4 right, 4 left

Green
16 "E" pieces–8 right, 8 left
8   "B"–4 right, 4 left

Pink
16 "E"–8 right, 8 left

Brown
16 "D"–8 right, 8 left
16 "A"–8 right, 8 left
24 "E"–12 right, 12 left

Beige
16 "C"–8 right, 8 left
24 "E"–12 right, 12 left

Patterned Light Brown
32 "E"–16 right, 16 left

Ivory
16 "E"–8 right, 8 left

Brown **Beige** **Green** **Patterned Brown** **Pink** **Purple** *Ivory*

2. This quilt is assembled in eight vertical strips, each representing the right or left half of one "point" in the design. Be sure to assemble the right and left halves so that the colors will line up. Attach them, from the top down, in this order:

A brown "D"
A beige "C"
A green "B"
A brown "A"
The "E" pieces:
    patterned brown
    beige
    green
    brown
    purple
    patterned brown
    beige
    pink
    ivory
    patterned brown
    brown
    green
    beige
    brown
    ivory
    purple
    patterned brown
    pink
A brown "A"
A purple "B"
A beige "C"
A brown "D"

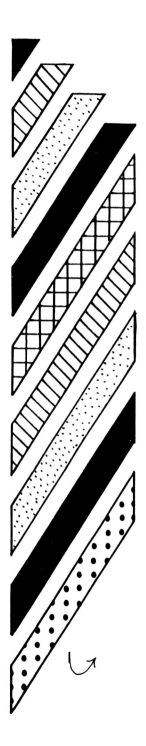

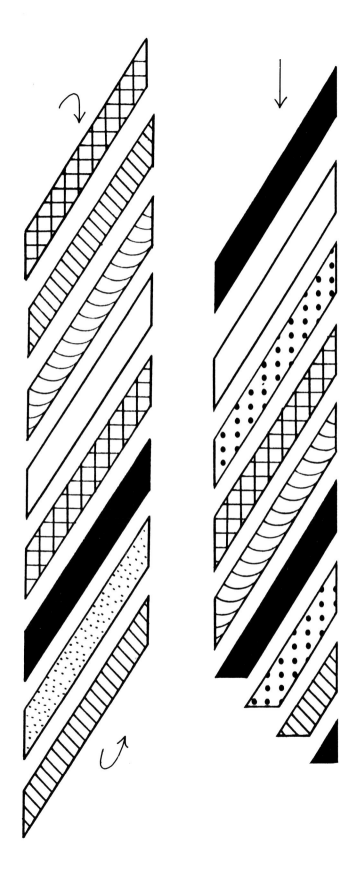

3. Attach the right and left halves of each "point" and sew the four points together to form the quilt top. Be very careful to line the colors up exactly.

4. Cut the backing fabric into two 3$\frac{1}{4}$-yard lengths. Sew them together along their long sides.

5. Pin and baste the back, batting, and top. Quilt along the outlines. Bind. Remove basting stitches.

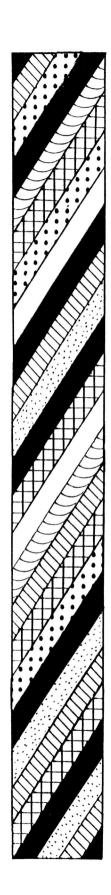

3.

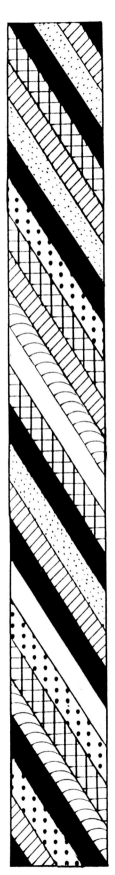

Pattern Pieces

Shown quarter-size unless otherwise noted

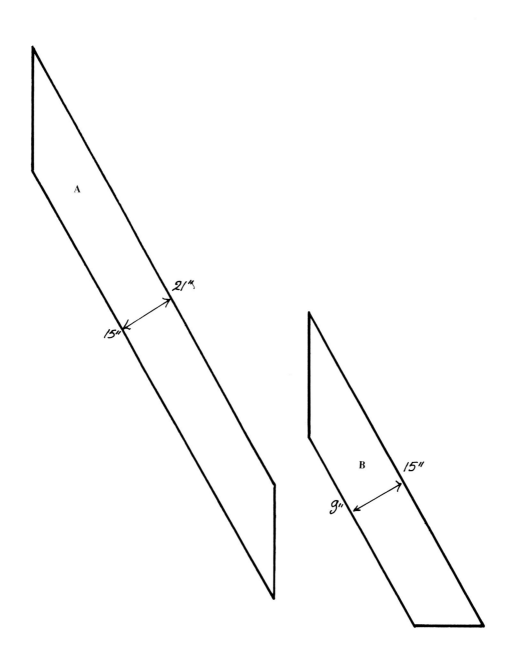

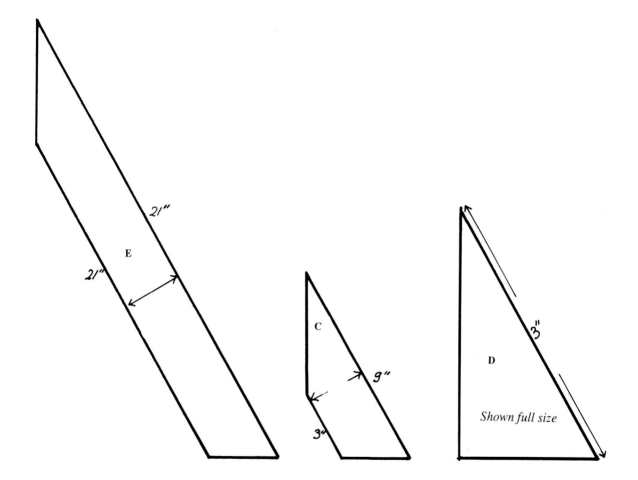

21″

21″

E

C

9″

3″

3″

D

Shown full size

Vital Statistics

Maker: Kirstin Olsen
Length: 108" (275 cm)
Width: 96" (244 cm)
Fabric Requirements: (45" or 114 cmwide)
2¹/₂ yards (2.3 m) red fabric
6 yards (5.5 m) black fabric
8 yards backing fabric
bias binding or 1 extra yard black fabric
Binding: bias bound

Instructions

1. Cut all pieces. You will need:

Black
2   96" x 27" panels
32   1" x 12" strips
192 2" x 2" squares

Red
16   4" x 12" strips
16   6" x 12" strips
16   2" x 12" strips
16   1" x 12" strips
160 2" x 2" squares
64   2" x 4" strips
32   2" x 6" strips

The overall pattern for the quilt in this project is adapted from one found on a common type of Navajo woman's garment. The quilting design is adapted from an ancient Pueblo pottery motif created near Mimbres, New Mexico.

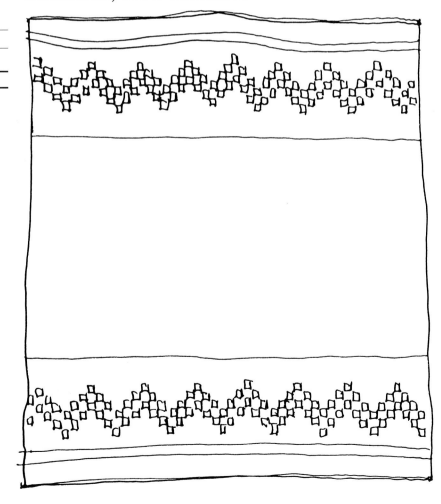

2. Assemble the checkerboard units as shown.

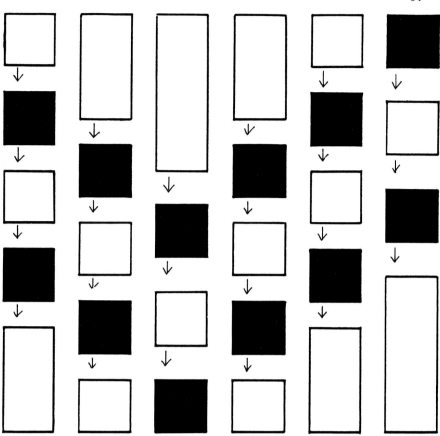

2.

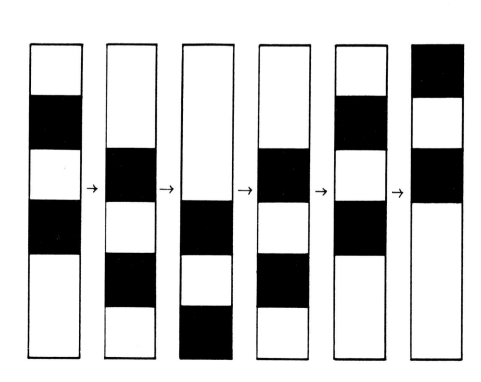

3. Sew two rows of eight checkerboard units each.

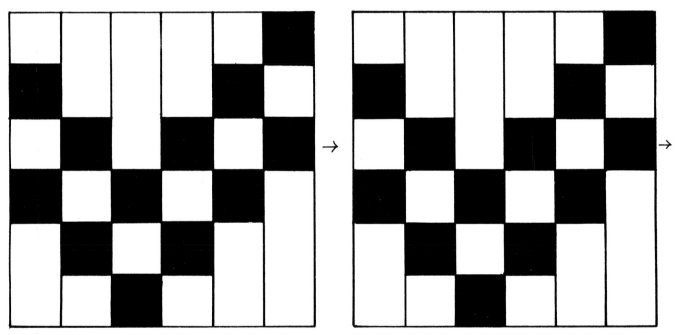

3.

(Only two of eight checkerboard units shown in this drawing.)

4. Assemble the border rows by sewing together:

    2 rows of eight 4" red strips
    4 rows of eight 1" black strips
    2 rows of eight 1" red strips
    2 rows of eight 2" red strips
    2 rows of eight 6" red strips

5. Make both borders by sewing, from the outside to the inside:

    a 4" red row
    a 1" black row
    a 1" red row
    a 1" black row
    a 2" red row
    a checkerboard row
    a 6" red row

6. Make the center panel by sewing the two large black panels together along their 96" sides. Sew the center panel between the two borders.

7. Cut the backing fabric into three $2\frac{2}{3}$-yard lengths. Sew them together along their $2\frac{2}{3}$-yard sides.

8. Pin and baste together the back, batting, and top. Quilt along the outlines of the borders and at 2" intervals along the 6" red band. Quilt five horizontal lines at 2" intervals on each side of the horizontal panel near the border. Then quilt one more line at a 1" interval. There should now be a 32" x 96" unquilted space. Divide it into three 32" squares and use the Mimbres pottery pattern to quilt the center.

9. Bind and remove basting stitches.

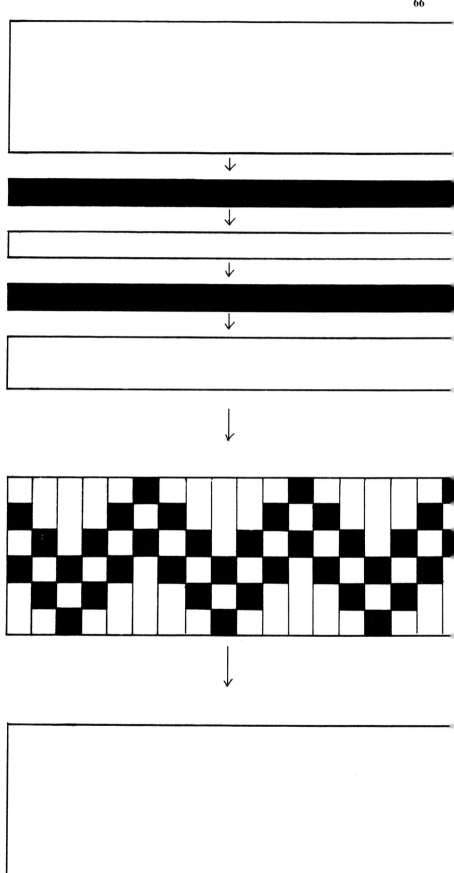

5.

Pattern Pieces
Shown half-size

1" X 12"

2" X 2"

4" X12"

6″X12″

2″X 12″

2″X4″

2″X 6″

Quilting Pattern

16"

SOUTHWEST TRIANGLES 7

This unique quilt makes a good wall hanging or a drape for a sofa. It was created for Concord Fabrics using Concord's Southwest line. If these exact fabrics are unavailable, of course, substitutions can be made.

Vital Statistics

Maker: Anne Boyce
Length: 31" (79 cm)
Width: 55½" (141 cm)
Fabric Requirements: (45" or 114 cm wide)

¼ yard (.25 m) red fabric (may have a pattern if desired)
¾ yard (.7 m) red striped fabric (stripes must run horizontally–parallel to the selvages–for the end result to match the quilt in the picture)
½ yard (.45 m) black fabric (may have a pattern
¼ yard (.25 m) teal fabric (plain or with a medium-sized pattern)
¼ yard (.25 m) plain or horizontally striped teal fabric.
2 yards (1.85 m) teal fabric with a small pattern

Binding: Self-bound

Instructions

1. Cut all pieces. You will need:

Red
6 large triangles

Striped Red
40 small triangles. Cut in pairs (A and B) as shown in the diagram so that the stripes line up in each pair. If, as in this quilt, the stripes are of different colors, make sure that they match in every triangle.
2 27³/₄" x 2" strips
2 27³/₄" x 1³/₄" strips

Black
48 small triangles.

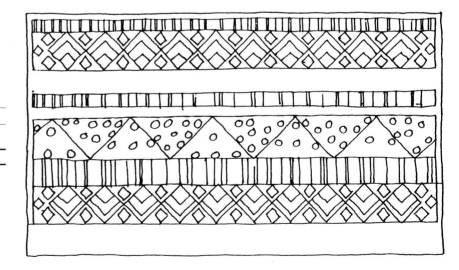

Teal (plain or striped)
2 27³/₄" x 3½" strips

Teal (plain or medium pattern)
6. large triangles

Teal (small pattern)
1 34" x 58½" backing piece
2 27³/₄" x 1³/₄" strips
4 27³/₄" x 3" strips

2. Assemble the top row:

Sew two 3"-wide teal strips together on their short sides to form one 55$\frac{1}{2}$" strip.

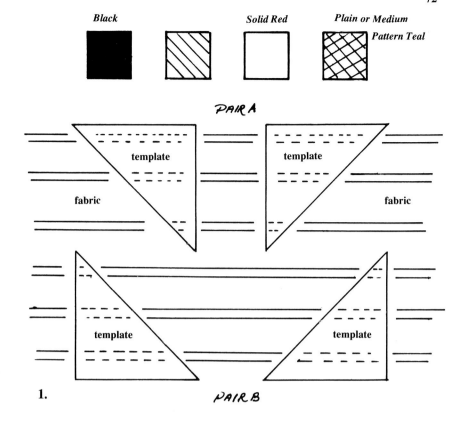

Black Solid Red Plain or Medium Pattern Teal

PAIR A

template template

fabric fabric

template template

1. PAIR B

3. Assemble the second row:

(a and b) Make nine squares by joining black and striped red triangles as shown.

(c) Make the tenth and eleventh squares, the end squares, by using three black triangles and only one red.

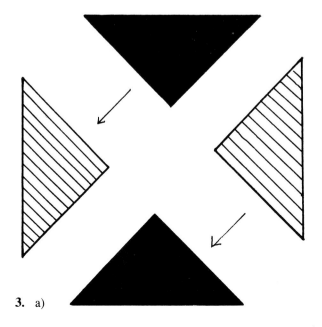

3. a)

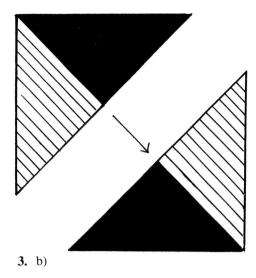

3. b)

3. c)

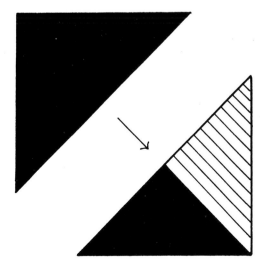 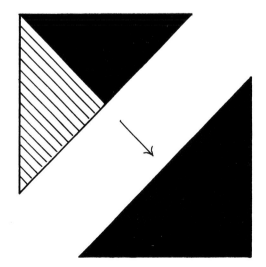

(d) Join the squares along their red
sides to make a long row. Be
especially careful to make sure that
the stripes match up!

3. d)

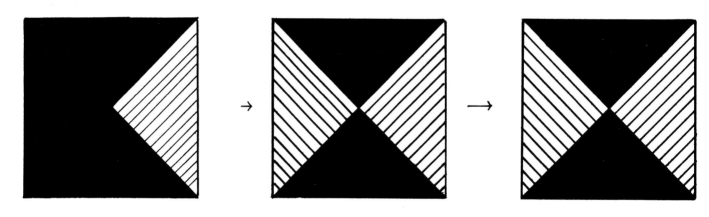

4. Assemble the third row:

Sew the two plain or striped teal strips together along their short sides.

5. Assemble the fourth row:

Sew the large red and teal triangles together along their 8" sides. This row will be longer than 55$\frac{1}{2}$".

5.

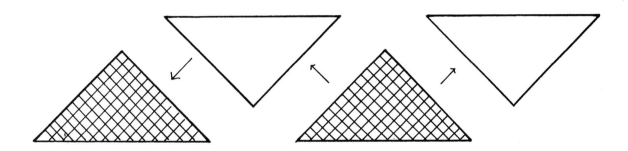

6. Assemble the fifth row:

Sew the two 1$\frac{3}{4}$"-wide teal strips together at their short ends.

7. Assemble the sixth row:

Sew the two 2"-wide striped red strips together at their short ends.

8. Assemble the seventh row:

Sew the remaining two teal strips together at their short ends.

9. Assemble the eighth row exactly as you did the second.

10. Assemble the ninth row:

Sew the last two red striped strips together at their short ends.

11. Join all the rows from top to bottom. Center the fourth row as you like and trim the sides so that they match the rest of the rows.

12. Pin and baste the top, back, and batting. Leave 1$\frac{1}{2}$" of backing on every side. Outline-quilt. Remove basting stitches.

Bind by folding each backing margin so that the raw edge meets the quilt. Fold again and stitch. Mitre the corners.

Pattern Pieces
Shown quarter-size unless otherwise noted

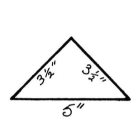

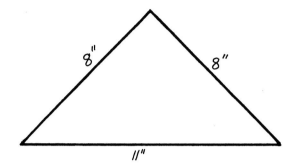

$3\frac{1}{2}'' \times 27\frac{3}{4}''$

$1\frac{3}{4}'' \times 27\frac{3}{4}''$

$2'' \times 27\frac{3}{4}''$

$3'' X 27\frac{3}{4}''$

$34''$

Shown one-eighth of full size $58\frac{1}{2}''$

THUNDERBIRD 8

Birds are a popular subject in Native American art. This particular fellow makes a dramatic addition to the walls of any room or entranceway. Double the dimensions of each piece to create a full-sized quilt. Be advised, however, that appliqué plays a central role in the construction of this project; this is easily the most complex quilt in this book.

Vital Statistics

Maker: Kirstin Olsen
Length: 47" (120 cm)
Width: 38¹⁄₂" (98 cm)
Fabric Requirements: (45" or 114 cm wide)

1¹⁄₃ yards (1.2 m) tan fabric
1¹⁄₃ yards (1.2 m) backing fabric
¹⁄₄ yard (.25 m) ivory fabric
³⁄₄ yard (.7 m) black fabric
¹⁄₃ yard (.3 m) assorted brown fabrics
   (Patterned fabrics made by
   Concord Fabrics were used in this
   quilt; if you cannot find these
   specific patterns, others may of
   course be substituted.)
bias binding or ¹⁄₂ yard brown fabric

Binding: bias binding

Instructions

1. Cut all pieces. You will need:

Ivory
2   A pieces, one right and one left
    (flip template over)
2   P (top wing band)
2   K (tail feather)
1   E (chest band)
8   Q (wing terrace)

Black
8   R (wing spots)
2   I (tail), one right and one left
2   B (neck chevron), one right and
    one left
2   D (shoulder), one right and one
    left
2   AA (wing feathers), one right and
    one left
2   G (waistband), one right and one
    left
2   M (wing arc), one right and one
    left

2   each: S, T, U, V, W, X, Q (wing
    terrace background)
2   Y (middle wing band)
1   BB (beak)
2   CC (outside wing band)
2   DD (lower outside band)
2   EE (inside wing band)

Brown
1   F (chest)
2   J (tail feather), one right and one
    left

2   H (lower section), one right and
    one left
2   N (inside of wing arc), one right
    and one left
1   L (eye)–here a fabric with
    conveniently placed spots was
    used; if your fabric is plain,
    embroider the pupil of the eye as
    the last step in the assembly of the
    appliqué

1 L (eye)–here a fabric with
   conveniently placed spots was
   used; if your fabric is plain,
   embroider the pupil of the eye as
   the last step in the assembly of the
   appliqué

2 Z (tail drip), one right and one left

2 C (neck), one right and one left

1 D (tail feather)

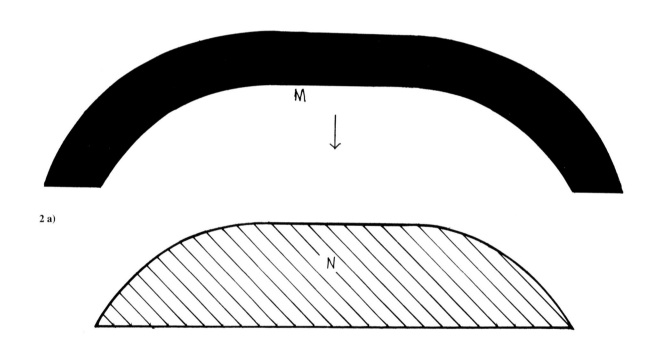

2 a)

2. Assemble the wings:

(a) Join inside wing arcs (N) to wing
arcs (M).

(b) Make the mid-wing terrace by sewing four horizontal rows as shown and joining the rows. Be sure to make a "left" wing terrace and a "right" terrace. When the bird is assembled, the ivory section, which is off-center on the black "background," should be closer to the outside of the wing than to the bird's body.

(c) Appliqué the R pieces onto the ivory terrace as shown.

(d) Sew the top wing band (P) to the top of the terrace section. Sew the outside wing band (CC) to the outside of the terrace section. Sew the three wing bands together, placing a brown band on either side of the black band.

2. b

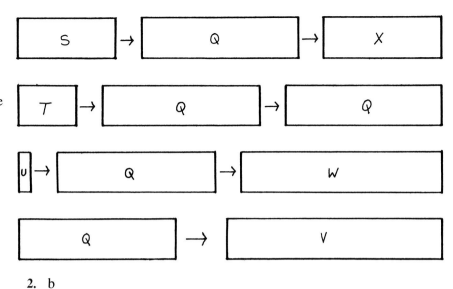

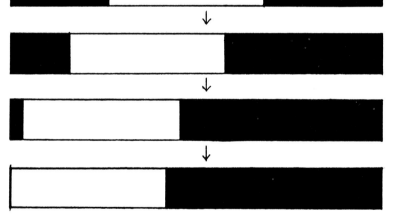

2 c)

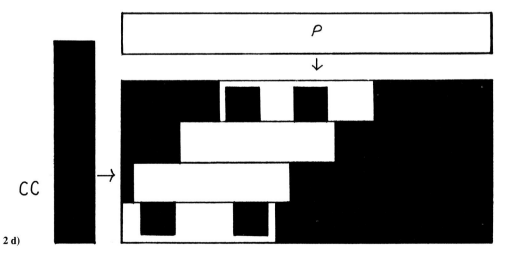

2 d)

(e) Join the terrace section, the wing band section, and the wing.

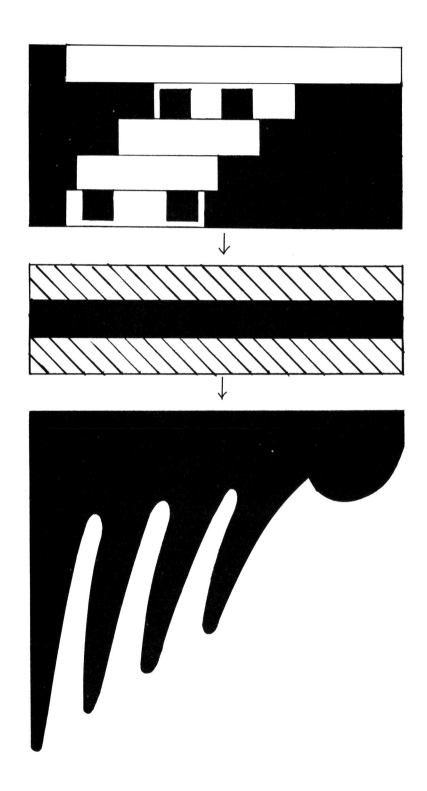

2. e)

(f) Attach the inside wing band (EE)
to the inside of this assembly and the
lower outside band (DD) to the
bottom of EE. Sew the wing arc
section to the top of the wing.

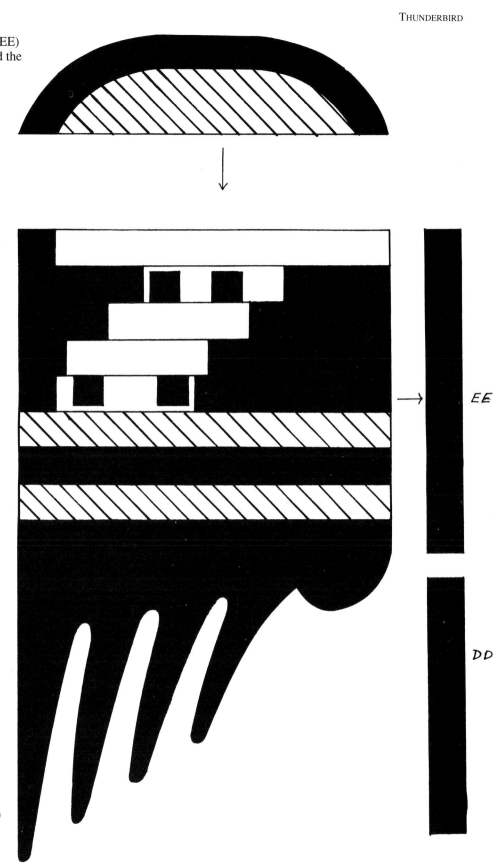

EE

DD

2.   f)

3. Assemble the tail section:

(a) Sew one tail drop (Z) to the inside curve of each tail (I).

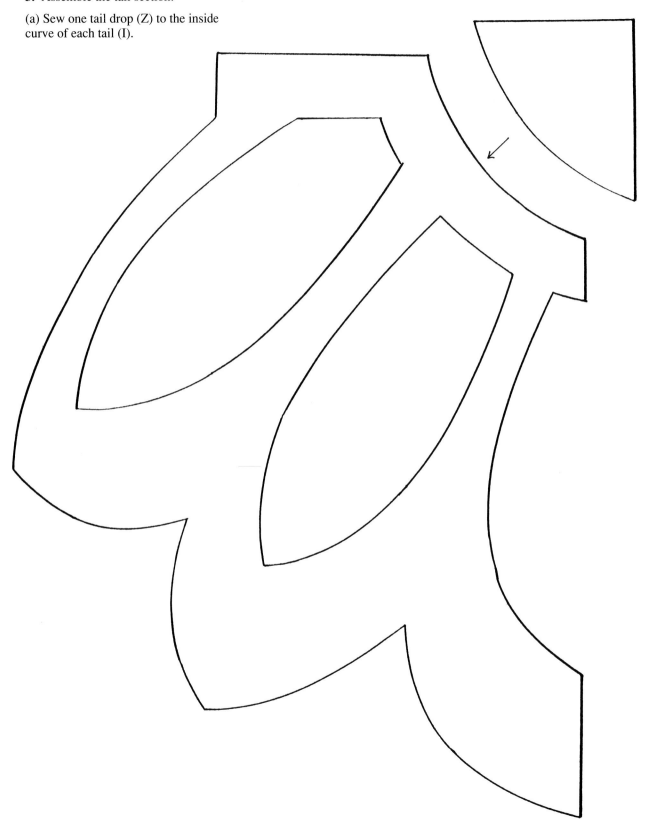

(b) Sew the two tail halves together.

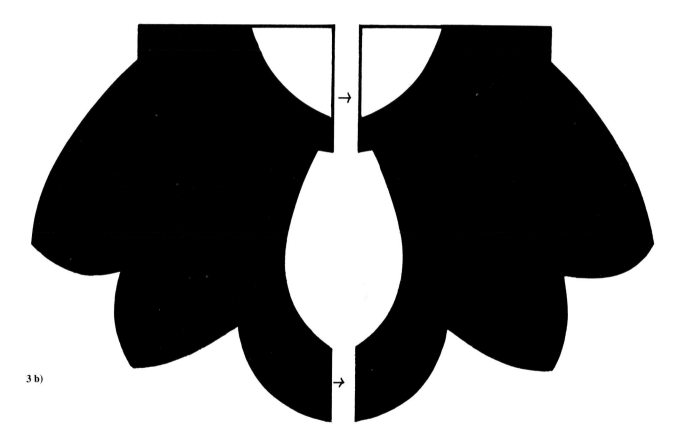

3 b)

(c) Appliqué the tail feathers (O, K, and J) onto the tail section.

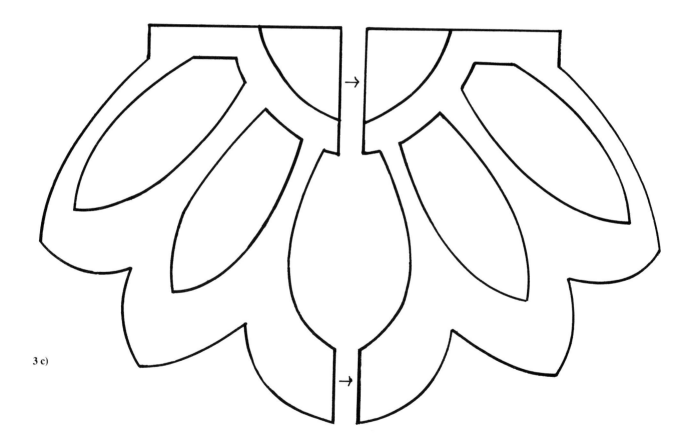

3 c)

4. Assemble the head and shoulders:

(a) Sew a neck section (C) to a neck chevron (B).

(b) Join the other side of the chevron to a head piece (A).

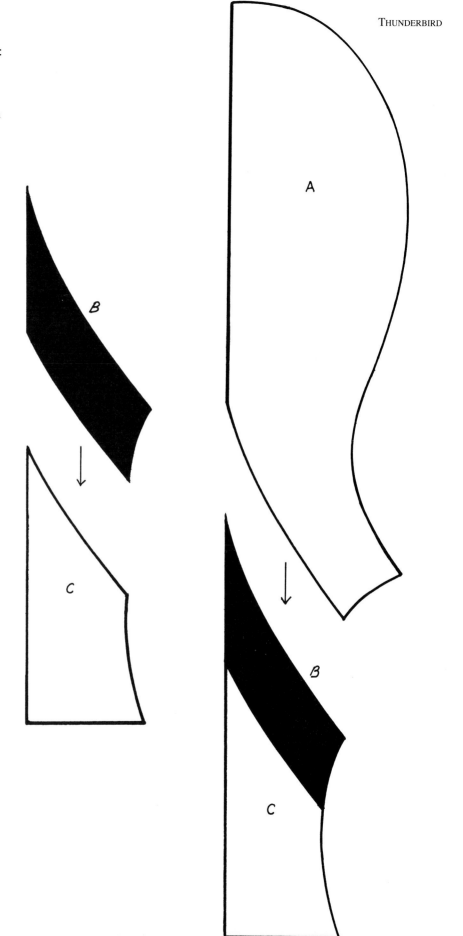

(c) Attach these pieces to a shoulder
(D).

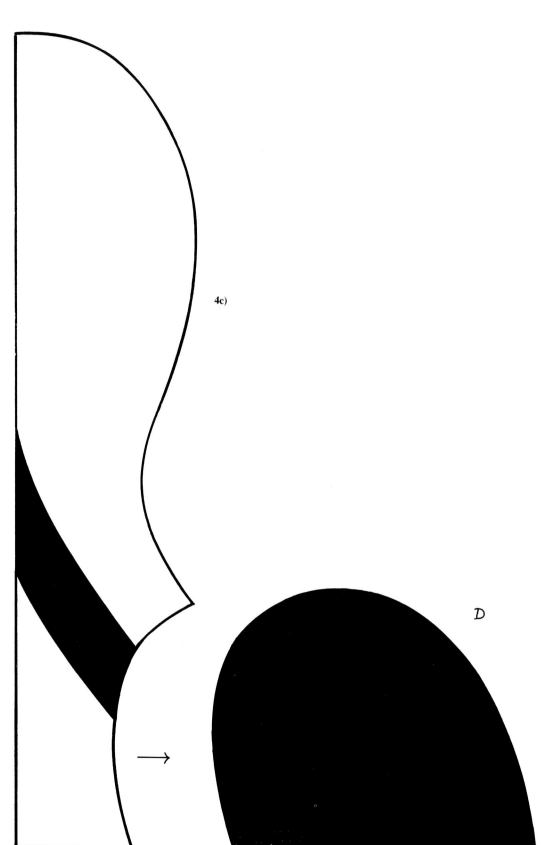

4c)

D

(d) Sew the two halves of the head
together and attach the beak (BB) to
one side. Appliqué the eye (L) on the
same side.

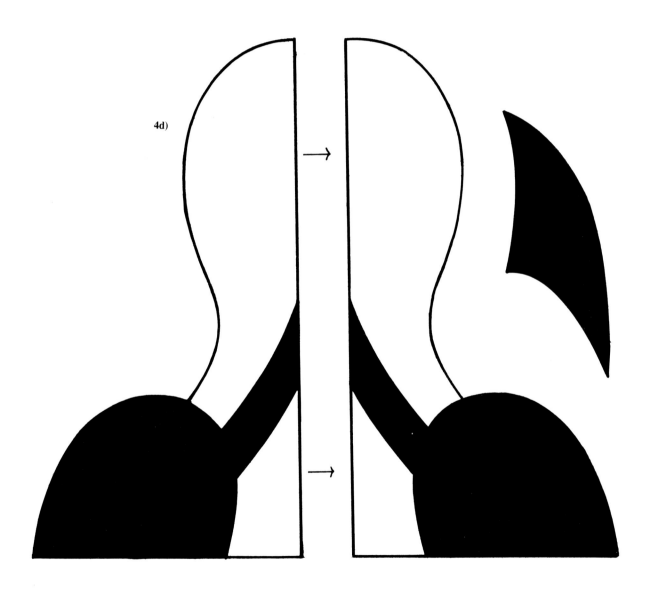

5. Assemble the midsection:

(a) Sew the chest band (E) to the top of the chest (F).

(b) Sew a waistband (G) to the top of each lower section (H).

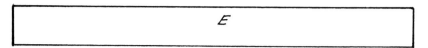

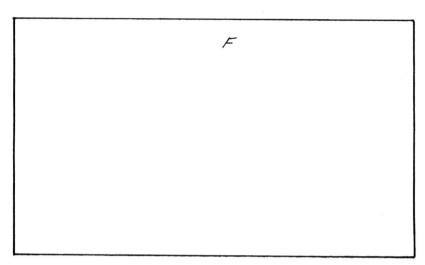

5. a

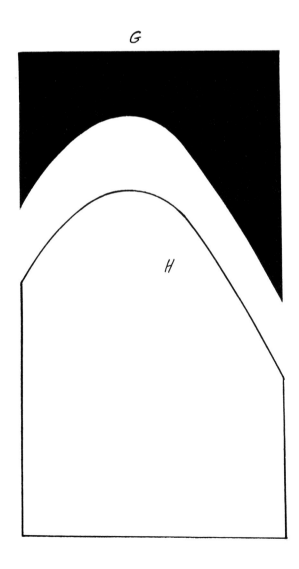

5. b

(c) Join the two halves so that the longer points on the waistband touch.

(d) Join the waistband to the chest.

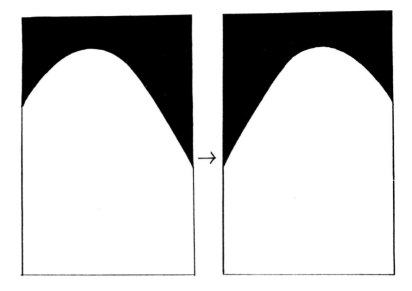

5. c)

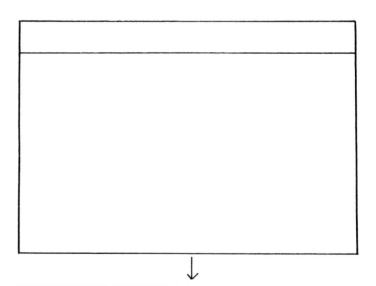

5. d)

6. Join the head section to the chest band. Attach one wing to each side. Finally, sew the tail section to the bottom. Clip as needed around curves and appliqué the entire bird to the tan fabric. If you need to embroider the pupil on the bird's eye, do so now.

7. Pin and baste top, batting, and back. Outline quilt the bird itself and quilt at one-inch intervals from the bird to the quilt edge, radiating outward. Remove basting stitches. Bind.

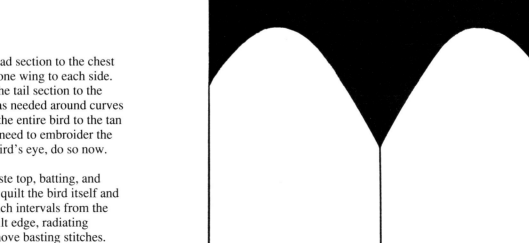

Pattern Pieces

Shown full size unless otherwise noted

Shown half-size

Shown half-size

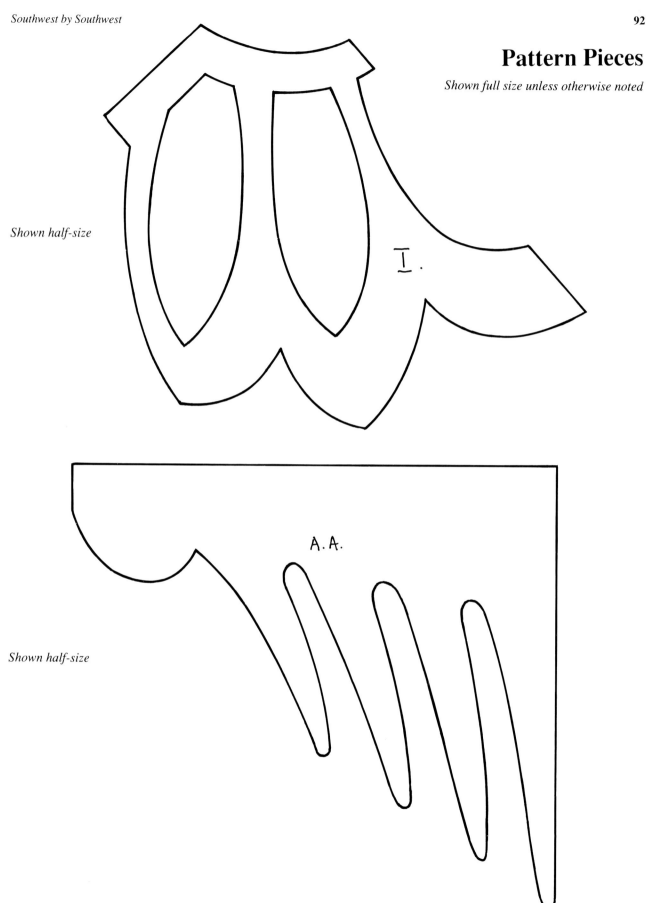

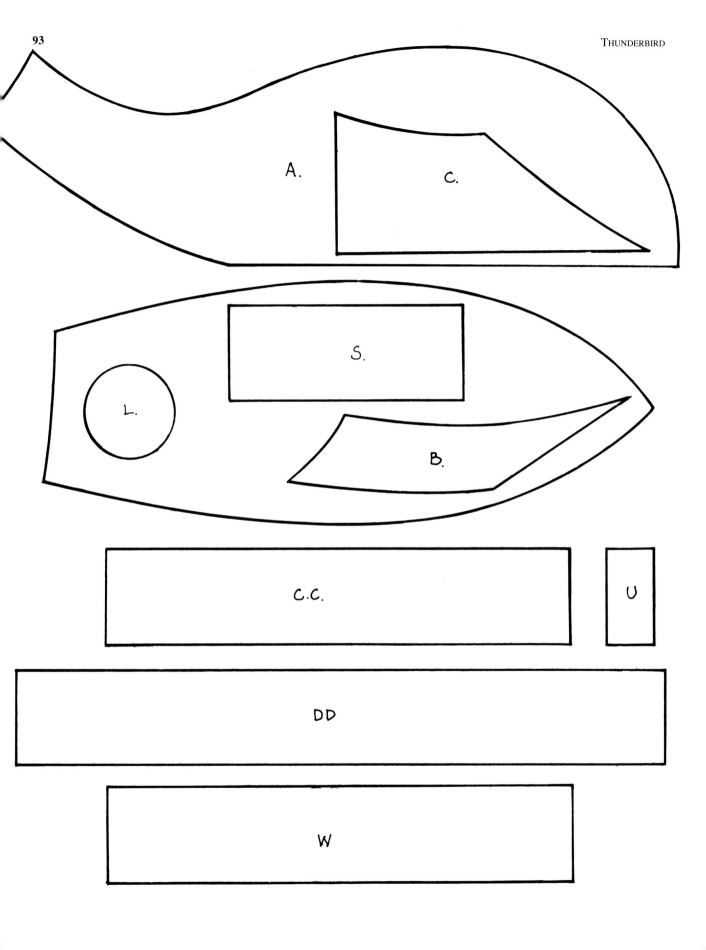

EE.

E.

N.

J.

BB.

V.

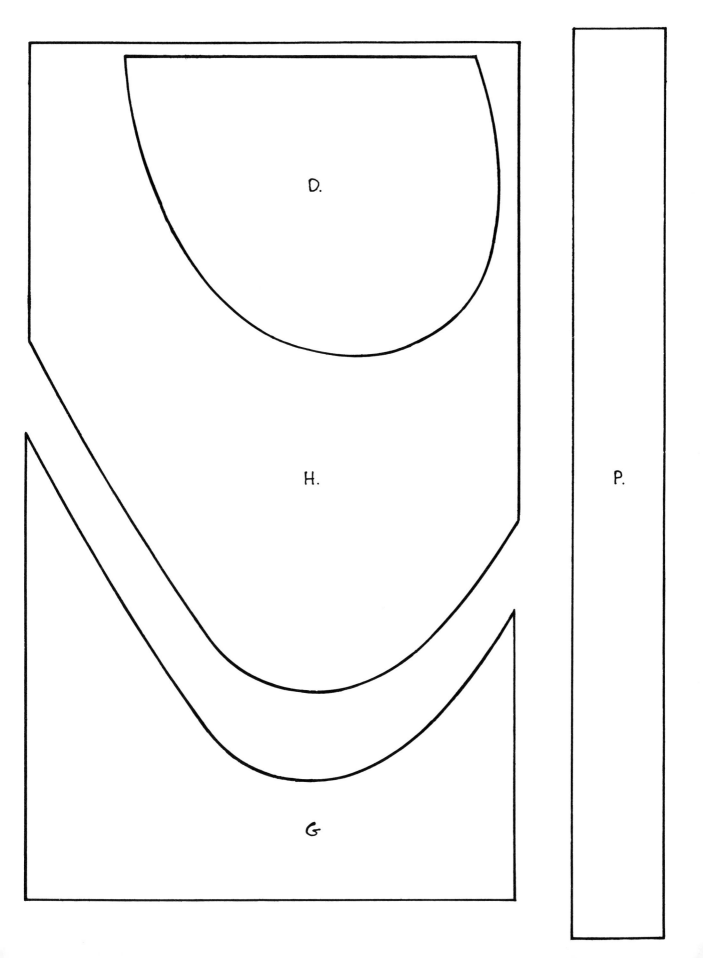

D.

H.

G

P.

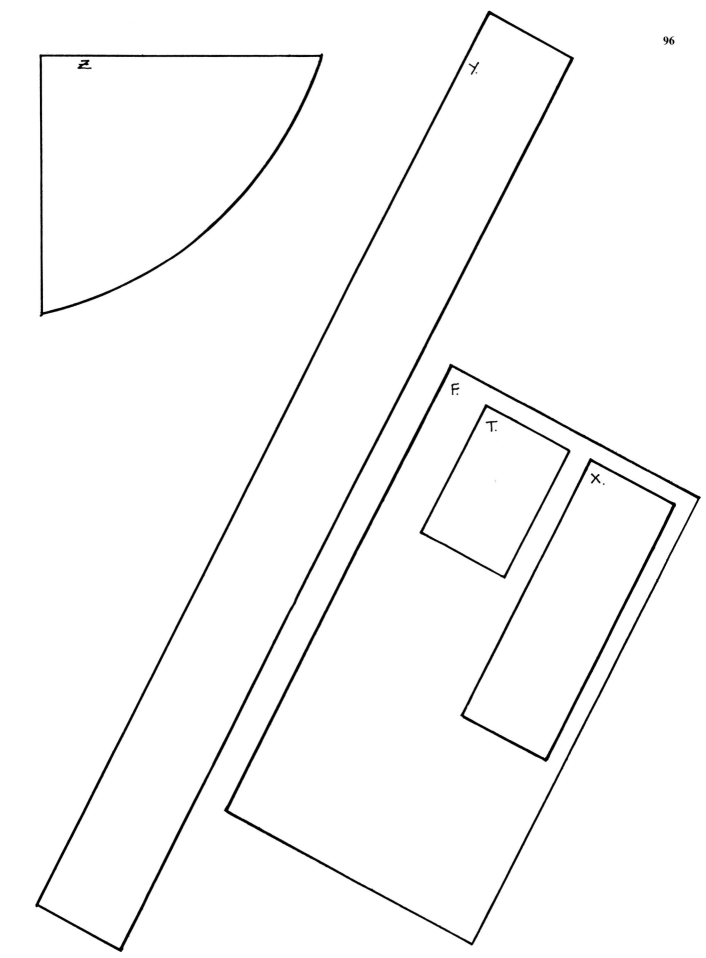

M.

O.

ZAPOTEC KEY　　9

Vital Statistics

Maker: Kirstin Olsen
Length: 94" (240 cm)
Width: 80" (203 cm)
Fabric Requirements: (45" or 114 cm wide)
4 yards (3.65 m) rust-colored fabric
5 yards (4.6 m) gold fabric
5¹/₃ yards (4.9 m) backing fabric
bias binding or 1 extra yard gold fabric

Binding: bias bound

Instructions

1. Cut all pieces. You will need:

Rust
160 2" x 2" squares
64 2" x 4" rectangles
32 2" x 6" rectangles
64 2" x 8" rectangles
32 2" x 10" rectangles

Gold
160 2" x 2" squares
64 2" x 4" rectangles
32 2" x 6" rectangles
64 2" x 8" rectangles
88 2" x 10" rectangles

The hook-shaped portion of this block is similar to a classical Greek design, but it's quintessentially Mexican as well. The terraced part of the design, too, is very characteristic of the Southwest. This particular pattern comes from stonework fashioned by the Zapotec, an ancient civilization of western Mexico.

2. Assemble 16 blocks in vertical strips as shown and join the strips. Assemble the remaining 16 blocks facing the other way by reversing the order of the strips.

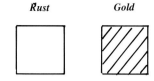

Rust   *Gold*

2.

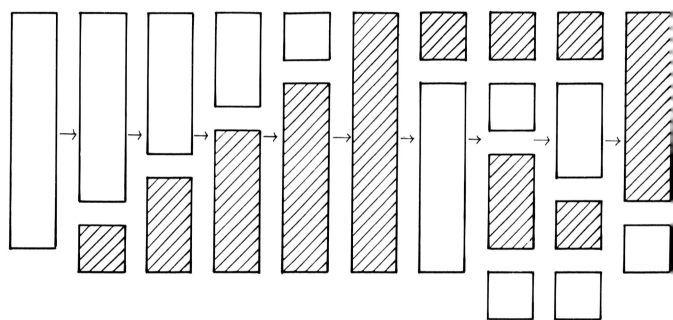

3. Assemble each row by joining four blocks which face the same way along their short sides.

4. Assemble the seven border strips by joining eight 10" strips along their short sides.

5. Finish the top by joining the rows of blocks, alternating rows that face right and rows that face left and placing a border strip between each row.

6. Pin and baste the top, batting, and back. Outline-quilt. Quilt the large gold space in each block as shown, starting in the top corner and stitching to the points indicated. Do the same for the large rust area.

Remove basting stitches. Bind.

Quilting Pattern

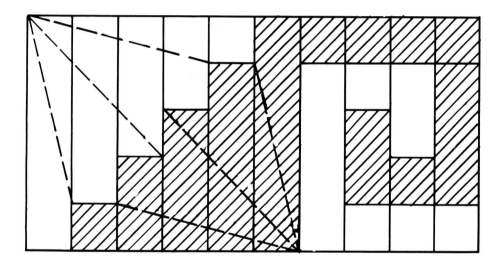

Pattern Pieces

Shown half-size

2"x10"

2"x8"

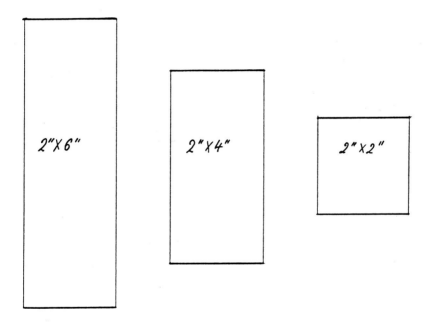

MIRROR IMAGE 10

Vital Statistics

Maker: Kirstin Olsen
Length: 66" (168 cm)
Width: 46" (117 cm)
Fabric Requirements: (45" or 114 cm wide)
2 yards (1.9 m) ivory fabric
1 yard (.9 m) turquoise fabric
1 yard (.9 m) apricot fabric
5 yards (4.6 m) backing fabric
bias binding or 1 extra yard ivory fabric
Binding: bias bound

Instructions

1. Cut all pieces. You will need:

Ivory
24 1" x 11" strips
6   1" x 2" rectangles
180 2" x 4" rectangles

Turquoise
48 3" x 4" rectangles
42 1" x 2" rectangles

Apricot
48 3" x 4" rectangles
42 1" x 2" rectangles

Taken from a Navajo rug design, this pattern is particularly dramatic when rendered in combinations of red, white, black, and gray. Here it is reproduced in softer colors in a size ideal for a small child's bed. For a full-size quilt, simply increase the dimensions of each piece by fifty percent.

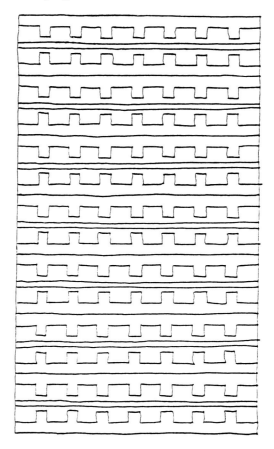

Ivory   **Turquoise**   **Apricot**

2. Assemble each row:

(a) Sew a 3" x 4" turquoise or apricot rectangle to a 2" x 4" ivory rectangle along the 4" sides. Repeat until there are eight such pairs.

(b) Sew a 1" x 2" turquoise or apricot strip to a 2" x 4" ivory rectangle along the 2" sides. Repeat until there are seven such pairs.

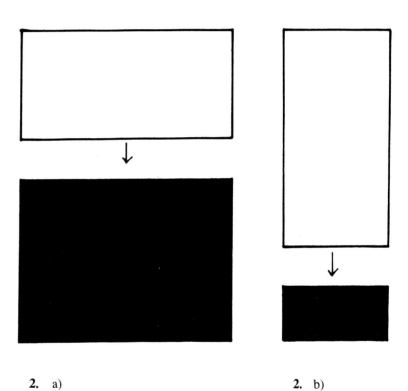

2. a)   **2.** b)

(c) Join the pairs, alternating. A 3" x
4" turquoise or apricot patch should
be on each end of the row.

Assemble the rest of the rows in the
same fashion.

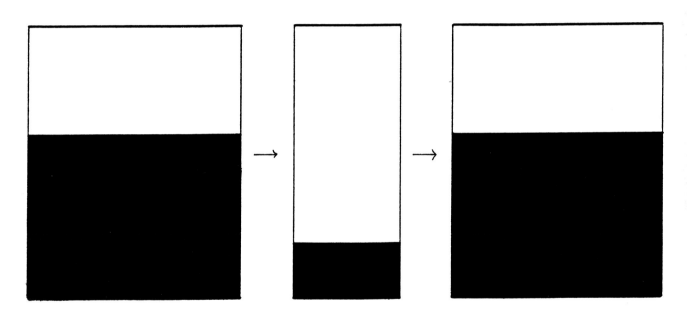

2. c)

3. Make each center row by sewing together four 1" x 11" strips and one 1" x 2" rectangle. Sew a turquoise row to one side of each center strip and an apricot row to the other.

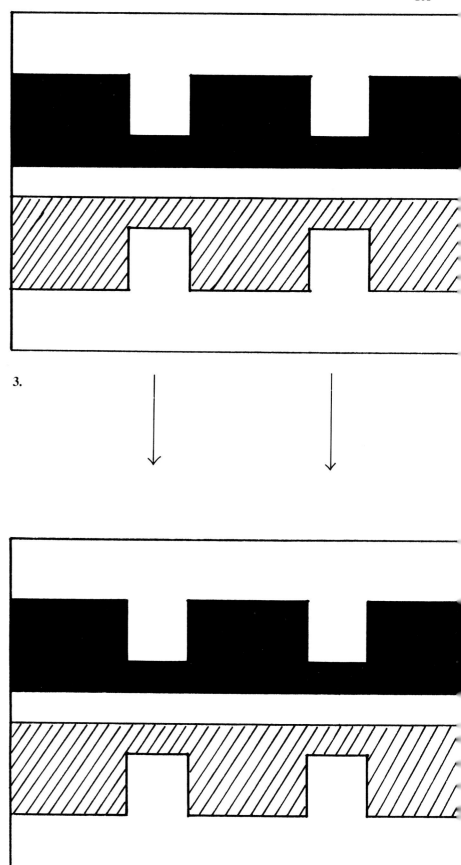

3.

4. Complete the quilt top by joining all six rows with the turquoise rows facing the same way.

5. Cut backing fabric into two 2$\frac{1}{2}$ yard lengths. Sew them together along the 2$\frac{1}{2}$ yard sides to form the back. Pin and baste the quilt top, batting, and back together. Outline-quilt and remove basting stitches. Bind.

Pattern Pieces
Shown half-size

1"X 11"

1"X2"

2"X4"

3"X4"

Vital Statistics

Maker: Kirstin Olsen
Length: 36" (91 cm)
Width: 38$^1/_2$" (98 cm)
Fabric Requirements: (45" or 114 cm wide)
$^1/_2$ yard (.45 m) light gray fabric
$^1/_4$ yard (.25 m) dark gray fabric
1$^1/_4$ yards (1.15 m) white fabric
$^2/_3$ yard (.6m) blue fabric
1 yard (.9m) backing fabric
bias binding or $^1/_2$ yard extra dark gray fabric

Binding: bias bound

Instructions

1. Cut all pieces. You will need:

Light Gray
44 full triangles

Dark Gray
22 full triangles

White
16 half triangles, eight right and eight left
104 full triangles

Blue
8 half triangles, four right and four left
52 full triangles

The design for this project is based on a willow basket made by a Chemehuevi artist. The Chemehuevi, who live in California and Arizona near the Colorado River, are renowned for their superb basketry. The colors used here remind some of the Southwest's famous turquoise jewelry and others of the brilliant blue Arizona sky.

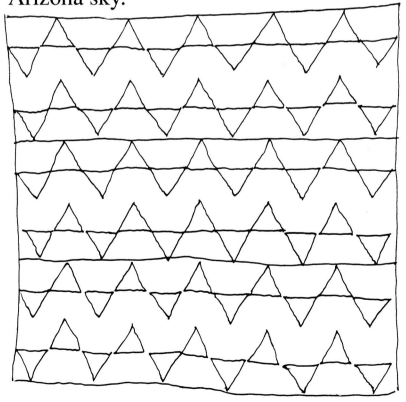

White **Light Gray**

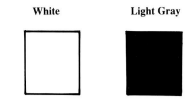

2. This quilt is assembled in horizontal rows, and there are only two types of rows.

(a) Row A is assembled as follows, from left to right:

a white half-triangle, a light gray triangle, three white triangles, one light gray, three white, one light gray, three white, one light gray, three white, one light gray, three white, one light gray, and one white half-triangle–a total of 23 pieces.

(b) Row B is also composed of 23 pieces, assembled as follows:

One white half-triangle, two white triangles, one light gray triangle, three white, one light gray, three white, one light gray, three white, one light gray, three white, one light gray, two white, and one white half-triangle.

ROW A

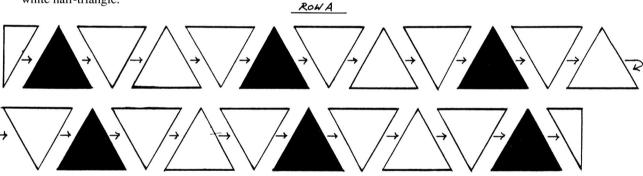

3. Assemble the top and bottom "blocks" of the quilt by joining, from top to bottom, an A row, a B row, an A row, and a B row.

Assemble the middle "block" in the same way, but substitute blue for white and dark gray for light gray.

Be especially careful to line up the points of the triangles.

4. Join the three blocks

5. Pin and baste the top, back and batting. Quilt with black thread between the "blocks" and along the lines indicated. Remove basting stitches. Bind.

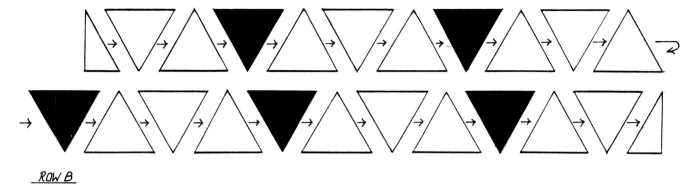

ROW B

Quilting Pattern

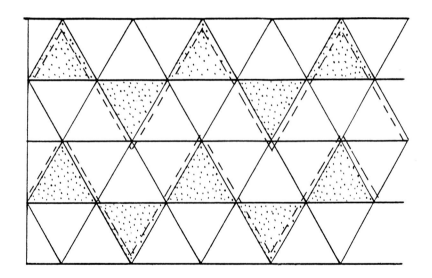

Pattern Pieces

Shown full size

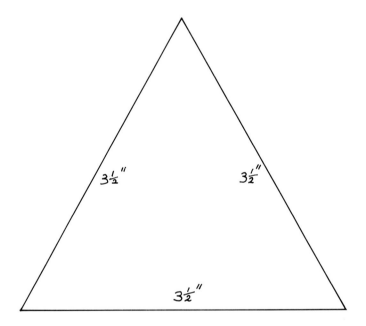

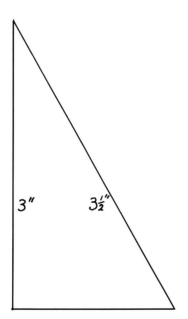

3" $3\frac{1}{2}$"

MEXICAN COLUMN 12

Vital Statistics

Maker: Kirstin Olsen
Length: 30" (76 cm)
Width: 33" (84 cm)
Fabric Requirements: (45" or 114 cm wide)
  ¾ yard (.7 m) green fabric
  1 yard (.9 m) black fabric
  1 yard (.9 m) backing fabric
  bias binding or ½ yard extra fabric
Binding: bias bound

The design for this project is taken from an ancient clay stamp found in Mexico City. Like Zapotec Key (chapter 9) it contains the classic hooks and stepped frets. This version is only a small wall hanging, but the pattern makes a fascinating full-size quilt as well.

Instructions

1. Cut all pieces. You will need:

Green
4 *1" x 11" strips*
40 *1" x 1" squares*
8 *1" x 2" rectangles*
16 *1" x 3" rectangles*
8 *1" x 4" rectangles*
16 *1" x 5" rectangles*
8 *1" x 6" rectangles*

Black
8 *1" x 11" strips*
48 *1" x 1" squares*
8 *1" x 2" rectangles*
16 *1" x 3" rectangles*
16 *1" x 4" rectangles*
8 *1" x 5" rectangles*
8 *1" x 6" rectangles*

2. Each block is assembled in vertical rows as shown. The rows, from left to right, consist of:

(1) a 1" x 11" black strip;
(2) a 5" green strip and a 6" black strip;
(3) a 1" green square, 3" black strip, 2" green strip, and 5" black strip;
(4) a 1" green square, 1" black square, 1" green square, 1" black square, 3" green strip, and a 4" black strip;

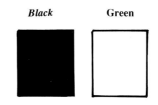

Black   Green

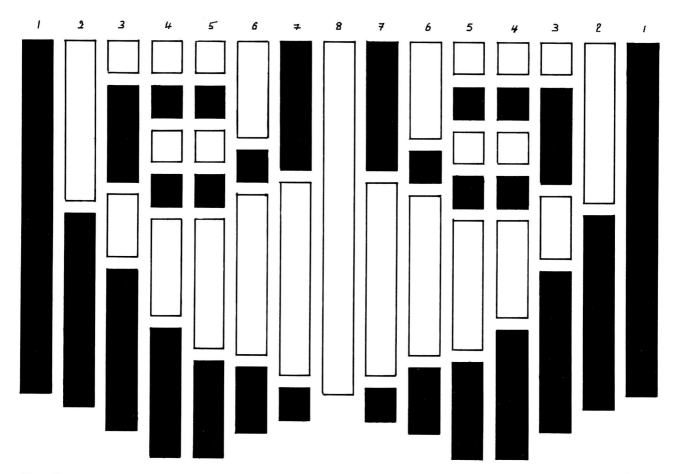

(5) a 1" green square, 1" black square, 1" green square, 1" black square, 4" green strip, and a 3" black strip;
(6) a 3" green strip, 1" black square, 5" green strip, and a 2" black strip;
(7) a 4" black strip, a 6" green strip, and a 1" black square;
(8) an 11" green strip.

    Rows 7 through 1 then repeat as indicated on the diagram.

2.

3. Pin and baste the top, batting, and
back. Outline–quilt and remove
basting stitches. Bind.

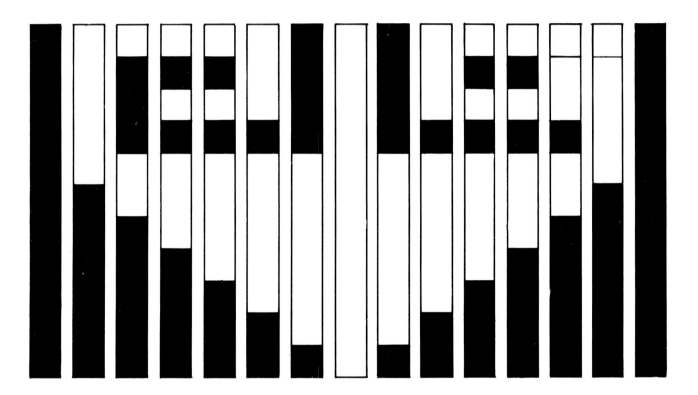

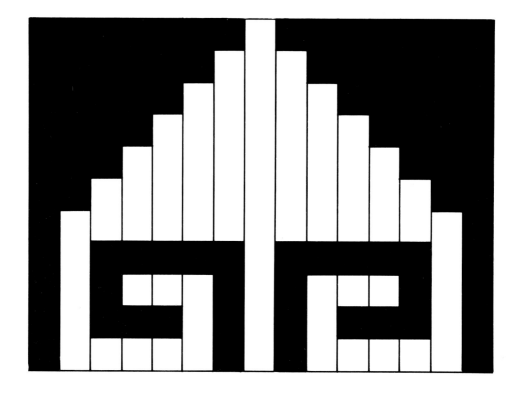

Pattern Pieces

Shown full size unless otherwise noted

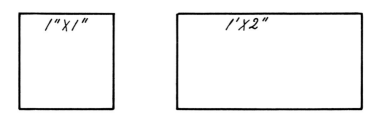

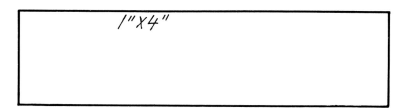

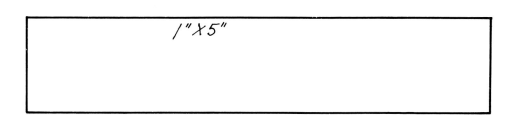

Metric Equivalents

INCHES TO MILLIMETRES AND CENTIMETRES

MM—millimetres   *CM—centimetres*

Inches	MM	CM	Inches	CM	Inches	CM
⅛	3	0.3	9	22.9	30	76.2
¼	6	0.6	10	25.4	31	78.7
⅜	10	1.0	11	27.9	32	81.3
½	13	1.3	12	30.5	33	83.8
⅝	16	1.6	13	33.0	34	86.4
¾	19	1.9	14	35.6	35	88.9
⅞	22	2.2	15	38.1	36	91.4
1	25	2.5	16	40.6	37	94.0
1¼	32	3.2	17	43.2	38	96.5
1½	38	3.8	18	45.7	39	99.1
1¾	44	4.4	19	48.3	40	101.6
2	51	5.1	20	50.8	41	104.1
2½	64	6.4	21	53.3	42	106.7
2	76	7.6	22	55.9	43	109.2
3½	89	8.9	23	58.4	44	111.8
4	102	10.2	24	61.0	45	114.3
4½	114	11.4	25	63.5	46	116.8
5	127	12.7	26	66.0	47	119.4
6	152	15.2	27	68.6	48	121.9
7	178	17.8	28	71.1	49	124.5
8	203	20.3	29	73.7	50	127.0

BIBLIOGRAPHY

Appleton, Le Roy H. *Indian Art of the Americas*. London & New York, 1950.

Coe, Ralph T. *Lost and Found Traditions: Native American Art 1965-1985*. New York: American Federation of Arts, 1986.

Covarrubias, Miguel. *The Eagle, the Jaguar, and the Serpent: Indian Art of the Americas*. New York, 1954.

———————— . *Indian Art of Mexico and Central America*. New York, 1957

Dockstader, Frederick J. *Indian Art in America: The Arts and Crafts of the North American Indian*. Greenwich, Conn.: New York Graphic Society, 1966.

Harmony by Hand: Art of the Southwest Indian, San Francisco: Chronicle Books, 1987.

Mora, Joseph. *The Year of the Hopi*. New York: Rizzoli Publications, 1979.

Sides, Dorothy Smith. *Decorative Art of the Southwest Indians*. New York: Dover Publications, 1961.

INDEX